I0485886

SOCIAL MEDIA

MASTER, MANIPULATE, AND DOMINATE

SOCIAL MEDIA MARKETING

FACEBOOK, TWITTER, YOUTUBE, INSTAGRAM, AND LINKEDIN

J. WOLF

© Copyright 2015 - All rights reserved.

In no way is it legal to reproduce, duplicate, or transmit any part of this document in either electronic means or in printed format. Recording of this publication is strictly prohibited and any storage of this document is not allowed unless with written permission from the publisher. All rights reserved.

The information provided herein is stated to be truthful and consistent, in that any liability, in terms of inattention or otherwise, by any usage or abuse of any policies, processes, or directions contained within is the solitary and utter responsibility of the recipient reader. Under no circumstances will any legal responsibility or blame be held against the publisher for any reparation, damages, or monetary loss due to the information herein, either directly or indirectly. Respective authors own all copyrights not held by the publisher.

Legal Notice:

This book is copyright protected. This is only for personal use. You cannot amend, distribute, sell, use, quote or paraphrase any part or the content within this book without the consent of the author or copyright owner. Legal action will be pursued if this is breached.

Disclaimer Notice:

Please note the information contained within this document is for educational and entertainment purposes only. Every attempt has been made to provide accurate, up to date and reliable complete information. No warranties of any kind are expressed or implied. Readers acknowledge that the author is not engaging in the rendering of legal, financial, medical or professional advice.

By reading this document, the reader agrees that under no circumstances are we responsible for any losses, direct or indirect, which are incurred as a result of the use of information contained within this document, including, but not limited to, —errors, omissions or inaccuracies.

TABLE OF CONTENTS

INTRODUCTION 7

PART ONE: THE STEP-BY-STEP GUIDE TO SOCIAL MARKETING .11

CHAPTER ONE: THE POWER OF SOCIAL MEDIA MARKETING 13

CHAPTER TWO: STEP ONE – IDENTITY AND CREATE THE
KEYWORD STRATEGY...29

CHAPTER THREE: STEP 2 – YOU HAVE TO OPTIMIZE YOUR
WEBSITE 39

CHAPTER FOUR: STEP 3 – CREATE A BLOG OR OTHER TYPE OF
CONTENT 57

CHAPTER FIVE: STEP 4 – PROMOTING CONTENT AND
PARTICIPATING IN DIFFERENT SOCIAL MEDIA 69

CHAPTER SIX: STEP 5 – CONVERT SITE TRAFFIC INTO THE LEADS
FOR YOUR BUSINESS 75

CHAPTER SEVEN: STEP 6- USE LEADS IN YOUR EMAILS WHEN
MARKETING...85

CHAPTER EIGHT: STEP 7- ENSURE THAT YOU ARE MOBILE
FRIENDLY 103

CHAPTER NINE: STEP 8- ANALYSIS AND REFINEMENT OF
STRATEGIES 109

PART TWO: SOCIAL MEDIA MARKETING 121

CHAPTER TEN: STEPS FOR IMPROVING THE CONTENT 123

CHAPTER ELEVEN: DOMINATE FACEBOOK MARKETING 129

CHAPTER TWELVE: DOMINATE TWITTER MARKETING 143

CHAPTER THIRTEEN:DOMINATE YOUTUBE MARKETING 159

CHAPTER FOURTEEN:DOMINATE INSTAGRAM MARKETING 173

CHAPTER FIFTEEN:DOMINATE LINKEDIN MARKETING 183

CHAPTER SIXTEEN: GENERAL TIPS ON USING SOCIAL MEDIA . 193

CHAPTER SEVENTEEN:ADVERTISING 209

KEY HIGHLIGHTS 225

CONCLUSION 235

INTRODUCTION

The days when small businesses could not effectively compete against large companies in the market because they could not afford to advertise their products or effectively brand themselves because of cost restrictions are long gone. Those were the days when advertising on TV and buying space on newspapers were the only effective marketing channels available. A lot has changed since then.

Advertising no longer works as it used to. You don't see big companies scampering to get their ads on TV, or hunt for billboards in the city. They now aim at reaching their customers the contemporary way. As you know, nowadays people get most of their news online, and conversations on the hottest topics take place in small online groups, forums, and website comment sections. Successful companies do not even need to jostle for space on radio or TV, and social media has emerged as the most powerful marketing tool there is. But then, you probably already know this, and the burning question is not what benefits social media brings, but how to use social media to harness all the benefits it offers to small businesses and large companies alike.

As a rule of thumb, you should not just dive into social media with the intent of marketing your products or building a brand; you need proper planning and a roadmap to achieve your end results. It's like going to an unknown city without a map and trying to explore all of it in one day. Does that sound feasible to you? You must first figure out how to execute your plan so that success will be guaranteed, and understand the downside to just jumping in. Many marketers today make mistakes that they never really recover from; you should not join this statistic.

What do you understand by the phrase *'social media'*? While the meaning may seem obvious, you probably have no specific definition of what it means. Social media refers to websites and applications that enable Internet users to create, access, and share a wide range of content, and to actively take part in social networking. Simply put, social media is a platform that allows users to communicate. This communication can take many forms, including adding comments, creating text, uploading videos and images, and interacting with what others have to share.

Social media includes social bookmarking, wikis, video and photo sharing, and social news, to mention just a few. The journey to establishing such a powerful and potent interaction platform has been long and intensive, but it is now ripe for you to take advantage of and reach the masses that are undeniably addicted to it. You will see its true potential very soon! If you are still unsure why you need to embrace social media as a marketing and branding platform, perhaps you need further illustration of just why it is the best place to find and engage your target audience and to ride the wave of engagement to make your business grow.

This book will be the comprehensive social media marketing guide you need to master, manipulate, and dominate social media, including Facebook, Twitter, Instagram, YouTube, and LinkedIn. The chapters herein are structured to make it easy for you to understand the why and the how of social media marketing, and to take you from a novice entrepreneur with no knowledge of social media to a marketing and branding guru capable of formulating and executing winning marketing strategies for profitable entrepreneurship.

Happy reading!

PART ONE

THE STEP-BY-STEP GUIDE TO SOCIAL MARKETING

This book will explain the various ways you can market on the social networking platforms that are available today. But you need to know how to ensure that you are at the top of Internet marketing. The first part of the book will help you understand what goes into Internet marketing.

There are certain steps that you need to follow in order to grasp the attention of the readers. The book will focus on teaching you these steps so that you can start on the right foot. We will split the steps chapter-wise so that you have a clear idea of what needs to be done when, and how. The chapters will make for easy reading for you. Most entrepreneurs are unaware of these steps, but there are also some experts who forget about these steps, too. This chapter is a beginning to the former, and a refresher to the latter.

CHAPTER ONE

THE POWER OF SOCIAL MEDIA MARKETING

I know you are ready to jump right in and start building a social media marketing campaign, probably on an improvise-as-you-go strategy, but hold on. Before you can start a successful marketing campaign on social media, it is important that you understand the wheels it runs on and get to know why so many people use it.

We can start with an in-depth definition of what it is before we proceed to unravel its mysteries. According to Wikipedia:

"Social media is online content that individual people create using highly scalable and accessible publishing technologies."

Further, it describes social media in its basic sense as:

"A shift in how ordinary people discover, digest and share news, content and information. Social media is a fusion of technology and sociology that transforms monologues (one-to-many) into dialogues (many-to-many) and can be considered a democratization of information that transforms ordinary content readers into content publishers."

Based on this elaborate definition, we can deduce that social media is a lot more than just different websites where individuals can post their thoughts and receive a handful of comments, likes, or shares. The collection of the many social media tools available today make one giant publishing platform where information is traded freely and everyone has the power to reach the masses. Wikipedia further describes social media as:

"An extremely popular platform that allows people to connect in an online world to form personal, political, and business relationships with information as the core uniting factor."

This extensive definition of social media can be broken down into several sections to allow us to understand exactly what it is, and to elaborate why it is such a potent communication and networking tool.

But our understanding of social media goes beyond any formal definitions. We know it as a very powerful tool that any company can use to increase their brand awareness and get more and more people to use their products. The power is simply impeccable and second to none!

THE HIERARCHY OF SOCIAL MEDIA MARKETING

The main issue with social marketing is that small business owners have begun to jump through the entire process without paying much heed to the hierarchy. There are quite a few large business owners who have also made similar mistakes. You will think that you are doing it right, but realize that you are actually making a very silly, rookie mistake that can cost you big. And until, and unless, someone pinpoints it for you and expressly tells you about it, you will not be able to take the steps to correct it and you will continue along the wrong path. It is always good to understand the hierarchy before stepping into creating new content for your website. The hierarchy for social media is in line with Maslow's Hierarchy for human nature. It is only when you achieve everything you need that you will reach the point of self-actualization. It is good for you to understand the hierarchy!

THE BLOG

This is the basic part of the hierarchy. It is also the simplest. I'm sure you know what blogging is and why it is used. You will also be aware of how one gets started on it and why we are listing it as the first step. Most marketers are familiar with this since they use it on a frequent basis. In the early stages it is always good to use a blog, since you will be able to advertise your business effectively to a small community of people on the Internet. You can treat it like a stepping stone. But before you begin your blog, it is best for you to understand what goes into creating blogs like yours based on the experience of seasoned marketers. This is your door to social marketing.

THE RSS

RSS is an acronym for real simple syndication. Most marketers use this technology. It is something that HAS to be used by every marketer. RSS means subscribing to other blogs and getting constant information on your home page. This will help you remain up to date about what others are doing and also seeing what is happening on your own page. Remaining up to date is extremely important, especially while on the Internet. You will be able to create new content around your products and services when you begin to use this technology. You will need to start out slow in order to learn how to use the technology to your benefit!

THE SOCIAL SEARCH

This is something that is ignored by most small business marketers. You forget that search engines use only the best websites when it comes to providing results to people who are looking for a particular type of content. It is essential to ensure that your page is on the top of the list provided by search engines, since that helps to increase your clientele. You must be aware of what SEO stands for. It means "search engine optimization" and is a very powerful tool to exploit on the Internet. It allows you to make use of certain important keywords that people will be looking for, and including them in your description will help you show up as the first result. There are websites that only advertise the best content available on the Internet. This is done by measuring the traffic that enters those websites. This advertisement is given the first position. To ensure that your advertisement is at the very top, you have to participate to manage your reputation.

SOCIAL BOOKMARKING

You will be able to open up new channels for yourself through social bookmarking. As you know, you can easily bookmark various pages on your computer. You don't have to have in-depth knowledge on it and can easily do it within a matter of seconds. But given the number of sites that you need to bookmark, it can get a little tiring and monotonous. You will find yourself participating on different platforms. You will also be able to gain a new audience. It does take a lot of effort and work on your part. But you have to try! This is the only way you will be able to master the art of networking on social media.

SOCIAL NETWORKS

There are multiple social networking websites that you can use to promote your products and services. The main focus of this book will be on these websites, and you have to follow the procedures that are explained in the latter part of the book if you are using social media for the very first time. Apart from creating a profile for your company, there are many other things that you must do and we will look at them one by one. You may find yourself frustrated by the amount of work it takes to ensure that you have good marketing, but remember that hard work does pay off! You will be able to ensure that you make a good number of sales. If you feel overwhelmed, then ask for help from friends or family.

MICRO

This includes platforms like Instagram and Twitter. These platforms help you track and join various discussions. You will have interactive sessions with your customers and can indulge in answering questions that they ask you. You will also be able to converse with your followers with ease. These are at the top of the pyramid since that implies that you have a foolproof business marketing strategy. Micro-sites are what many million-dollar companies make use of, not just to connect with their fan base, but also to improve their company's image. You will need to ensure that the content that is provided in these platforms is perfect!

THE COMPONENTS OF SOCIAL MEDIA

When you wish to understand something thoroughly, you must split it up into small pieces and study each of them individually. So, when you wish to understand social media thoroughly, you must start with its components and understand them bit-by-bit.

As you can see, there are three major components of social media:

SOCIAL MEDIA IS A PUBLISHING PLATFORM FOR EVERYONE

Unlike any other interaction platform in history, social media is an online location-independent channel whose content is generated by the users. Unlike TVs, newspapers, radio, and other traditional communication platforms, this platform is highly accessible and scalable to the public. This very aspect makes it one of the most accepted and most versatile forms of media and you will be surprised at how much your business will actually grow when you hand some of your power to the public. This means that, because it is easily accessible, the tools of social media are intuitive and simple enough for the common user to read, and to publish. Nothing is too complicated and you don't have to be a web expert to partake in its activities.

SOCIAL MEDIA IS A CHANNEL THROUGH WHICH INFORMATION IS DIFFUSED

Considered a modern-day information renaissance, social media can diffuse information faster and more efficiently than any other platform currently in existence. Imagine sharing a news article from Iceland and having it become an overnight rage in China. That is how versatile it is and the smallest bit of information can travel at the speed of light. This feature has made it a channel that has revolutionized how people find, read, and share information, such as news, media, and any other content that they deem to be important or informative. Social media, being a fusion of sociology and technology, now plays a large role in the business and marketing strategy for any serious business. Its limits are set only by the technology of social interaction tools.

SOCIAL MEDIA IS A PLACE TO BUILD RELATIONSHIPS THROUGH SHARING

Social media uncovered something about humans that no one knew before—the strength that hides in sharing information. Sharing has become an essential component in the explosion of social media. Through sharing of content, people now connect with others and empower them to become their own publishers in many ways. As was mentioned before, it does not matter where you are based. Just by making use of social media, you can connect to a large audience, which can lie next door or halfway across the world. If you have useful information, then there will be millions of takers for it! The myriad forms of relationships formed through sharing have enabled businesses, authorities and individuals to harness the power of social media to achieve their goals.

TOP REASONS TO ADOPT SOCIAL MEDIA MARKETING

Up to now, we have described the basics of social media and looked at three of its main components. Now let us look at the top reasons that make social media marketing such a rage, and what you will miss out on if you don't make use of it.

INCREASED BRAND RECOGNITION

For any company, increasing brand awareness is one of the most important aspects. It is vital that people know about you if you want them to buy from you. This is possible only if you make your presence felt on social media platforms. And if you are not yet on the web, then you are losing out on hundreds of customers. Any opportunity to increase your brand visibility and syndicate your content is valuable. Social media networks are open channels for your brand's voice and a way to share content with an audience without charge. This is essential because your brand becomes more accessible for new customers and more recognizable for existing customers.

IMPROVED BRAND LOYALTY

It is understood that ten new customers are equal to one old customer. This means that you have to do everything in your power to hold on to the customers that you have now, and that can be done through brand loyalty. A study by Texas Tech University established that brands that engage on social media enjoy greater customer loyalty than those that do not. The report concluded that companies that use social media to connect and interact with their audience morph their consumers into being loyal to their brands.

MORE OPPORTUNITIES TO CONVERT

Every post shared on a social media platform is an opportunity to convert a new audience into customers. If you have 500 people reading your post, chances are at least 40% of them will turn into customers. Now imagine what will happen if millions see it? So it is important to use social media to connect to an audience. A small business that builds a following will simultaneously have access to new, recent, and old customers, thereby getting an opportunity to interact with them all and convert them into loyal customers.

HIGHER CONVERSION RATES

Trust factor is big for any brand. In order to convert a reader into a customer, it is important to present them with something that will win their trust. The humanization element of social media is the most significant way that brands get to increase customer conversion rates. The best way that a brand can be more humanized is through interaction on social media where brands act like ordinary users do. The company will interact with the customers independently and increase loyalty. Compared to outbound marketing, social media has a 100% higher lead-to-close rate because followers tend to trust brands that have social representation. And these are not just numbers. There are various study results that back up these theories.

LOWER MARKETING COSTS

Marketing costs need to be accounted for, as you cannot have them pile up when you go about the marketing process. Many companies make the mistake of spending more than they can afford, and that is one habit that needs to be addressed. It can be resolved by making use of social media websites effectively. In a study conducted by Hubspot, 84% of marketers said that as little as five hours of effort per week is sufficient to generate significantly high traffic to a business website. Even paid advertising is relatively cheaper on Facebook and Twitter (depending on your goals). A small social media budget results in significant traffic and conversion when social media marketing is done right.

RICHER CUSTOMER EXPERIENCES

At its core, social media is an effective communication channel, just like telephone and email. Every interaction a company has with a customer on social media is an opportunity to demonstrate the quality of customer service, and to enrich the relationship the business has with the customer. Social media presents an opportunity for businesses to offer a personalized service experience to its customers.

These are just some of the advantages of using social media to enhance your business, but there are many more. Once you start using it, you will get acquainted with more of these advantages and understand its true worth.

CHAPTER TWO

STEP ONE – IDENTITY AND CREATE THE KEYWORD STRATEGY

When you have customers looking for something, you want them to reach your website, or advertisement, using a single word. That is what a keyword does. A keyword is essentially a word, or a phrase, that a person searches for in social networking platforms such as Google, Facebook, Twitter, LinkedIn, and YouTube. You have to know what keywords people will be searching for and incorporate them into your website. Then when they type the word in, and click search, they will find your page. This will mean that you are doing it right, but it is not as simple as it sounds. In this chapter, we will see how to identify these words and how you can incorporate them into your marketing strategy.

WHY SHOULD YOU BUILD A KEYWORD STRATEGY?

There are many consumers all over the world who are looking for businesses on search engines. They use a lot of effort to search for these businesses. But how do they do it? They use keywords. You, as a business owner, can use this to your advantage. You will need to ensure that your website revolves around the keywords that are in line with your line of business, and the words that your potential consumers may use. Think about it, in a sea of thousands, won't your customers be interested in looking for you in a straightforward manner? Or will they fancy using a complicated technique to look for you? They will obviously pick the former and you must help them in the process.

This will help you, since the chances of the potential consumers finding you will increase through the use of those keywords. This will enable your business to flourish. And that is not an exaggeration! You will benefit from it greatly and will see how your business goes from being small to being one that will cater to many people.

You may wonder how you can zero in on the keywords that are most common to your line of business. But there are techniques you can use to determine these keywords. However, you will need to be able to determine their popularity and competitiveness. Therefore, you must conduct tests and analyses to help you understand how effective various keywords are in attracting your potential consumers to your website.

This section will help you learn how to define keywords, which will in turn maximize the potential to draw prospective customers into your business through different social networks. You have to make use of the best words that will help them find you. The research to identify the best keywords is an ongoing process and you must make the effort to follow this closely. You will be able to gather valuable information on the trends of the industry, and the demand and supply of various products. If you conduct thorough research on keywords, you will be able to avoid spending extra money on different packages that help you advertise your products. You will also be able to improve the traffic to your website.

How to Build Your Keyword Strategy

When you wish to start out with keywords, you have to have a set strategy in mind so that it becomes easy for you to go about it.

This section provides you with the basic strategy that you can follow to build your set of keywords.

Identify a Minimum of Three Keywords

Think of your business from a customer's perspective. If you are a small business, you cannot expect your potential customers to know the name of your company. If you are a large business, you do not have to worry about the first keyword. However, you will need to come up with a list of words or phrases that define your business or your product as a whole. This will give you your list of three or more keywords. Since this is the very first step of the process, you must start out on the right foot. Do as much research on the topic as possible before you go about the process. See what other companies are doing and go about it the same way.

IDENTIFY THE KEYWORDS BASED ON RELEVANCE

There are certain keywords that you may zero in on in the above step, but you will have to check their relevance to your business and also the level of difficulty. There are many words, like marketing or business, that are very competitive. These words are difficult to rank in results produced by search engines.

If you are a small business, you will have to choose words that do not exhibit too much competition. These words must also be related to your business. These words are often known as the long tail keywords. A keyword that has a great amount of search on it is a competitive word. So trying to use these will mean that you are trying to compete with several people. That might slow you down or make the process more difficult for you. There are different tools that you can use to identify the competitiveness of keywords that you have settled on. This will also help you identify new words that you can use to benefit your business. The most common tools are the Google Keyword Tool and the HubSpot's Suggest Keywords.

The other important factor about choosing your keyword is the relevance of that keyword to your business. There are some keywords that are difficult to rank. But these words may or may not be relevant to your business. You can do a small search on Google and check words that are popular in your category. You have to strike a balance between the relevance of the keywords to your business and their level of difficulty. From the list that you create above, you should choose five keywords that match your business best. If you do not have that many, brainstorm and identify some more. You have to remember that these keywords need to be apt. You can always try new keywords to see which fits your business best. After all, your aim is to do as well as possible for your website.

LSI – Latent Semantic Indexing

Your website will appear on a search engine results page (SERP) only with the help of keywords. These primary keywords give an idea as to what your website is really about and when a searcher searches for those particular keywords, your website will pop up on the results page. To make your website more relevant, you can use LSI keywords. It is a method by which search engines determine whether your website has good content and is on-topic or if it is just spam.

Most people understand LSI keywords, or long tail keywords, as they are known, as mere synonyms for primary keywords. This might be true to an extent but it LSI keywords are more than that.

For example, let us take the term "teacher." This is a primary keyword but there are a million other websites, which use that keyword. LSI helps in making an educated guess by using the rest of the content and deciding what type of teacher is actually being discussed here. If your website makes use of terms like "keyboard," "music," "notes," etc., your website will appear in searches related to music teachers. Search engines know that words like "chord," "bass," "alto," etc., and other words closely related to music will appear in a good article. These jargon words are known as LSI terms.

When a searcher starts a search, the search engine reads your article and determines the keyword density by looking at the entire number of words in the article and finding out how many times particular words or phrases are repeated in the article. Words that are often repeated have a higher keyword density. Including these keywords in the title, first paragraph, and last paragraph of your article will help increase the keyword density, as the search engines put extra emphasis on these areas of the article. It then picks out the words with the highest keyword density and decides what the article is about. The search engine has a database of related terms of any keyword and if those related terms do not appear, it is given a lower relevancy score and is placed below others. Articles with higher relevancy scores will rank higher in the search engine's results page. Repeating the same phrases will not help but using synonyms can make a difference and give the reader content that is richer and legitimate.

DESIGN YOUR WEBSITE AROUND THESE KEYWORDS

Once you have narrowed down the list of your keywords to five, you then have to incorporate these keywords into your website. The main focus of this activity is to enable your website to be found. For this, you have to make use of these words in the best possible way. You will find out how to do this in the next step.

CHAPTER THREE

STEP 2 – YOU HAVE TO OPTIMIZE YOUR WEBSITE

You have made the list of keywords that you need to use for your business. You now have to ensure that you increase the ranking of those keywords to enhance the chance of attracting people to your website. Search engine optimization (SEO) is your savior! This is exactly what you will have to do for your business.

If you want to be viewed by your consumers, you will need to aim at being at the top, or somewhere on the first page of search results. If your potential customers are not satisfied with what they find in the first few posts, then they will quickly move on to the next few. And if you happen to be there, chances are they will visit you and like what you have on offer there. So don't underestimate the value of two or three spots below the first result. Once you land there, you can slowly climb higher and higher. The top spot is a coveted one, as most people will be keen on looking at what the first page has on offer. This spot is what all companies, big or small, are after. If this is not possible, you need to aim at being in the first few pages, say the first five, of the search. How many times have you moved to the second or third page when you haven't found whatever you were looking for? So, it will pay to make that effort and try to land on any one of the first five pages. Additionally, Google has advised most businesses to design their websites for their visitors, or potential customers, instead of for search engines. You need to keep this in mind in order to do well in the market. But before that, you will need to learn and understand what SEO is, and how it can help you optimize your website and search.

WHAT IS SEO?

SEO is an acronym for search engine optimization, which means optimizing your website to help you land the first spot or one of the first five spots in search results. There are two types of SEO; on–page SEO and off–page SEO. On–page SEO refers to the way in which you present your words on a search engine. You can work on improving this immediately, if necessary. Off–page SEO is a reflection of how strong your website is on the Internet. This is determined by what people on other websites say about your website. This is something that may take time to improve. Although on–page SEO only affects 25% of the ranking of your website, it is best to start off with this, since it can be improved very quickly. Let us work on improving on–page SEO for your company.

THE MAIN ELEMENTS OF ON–PAGE SEO

Regardless of whether you are already making use of this or not, this segment will look at some of the main elements of on-page SEO.

Since this is the easiest to clean up, you will learn how to do this. The steps that follow will help you identify what you must do. This section covers seven elements that play a major role in helping your website rise to the top of the search results on any search engine, or social networking platform.

THE PAGE TITLE

This is a very important part of the website. This is like the title of a book. Consider this for an example – you are walking past a bookstore and decide to walk into the store. You have the urge to walk up to the fiction aisle and look for a book that is worth reading. Would you pick a book that has the worst title possible? You would not. It is the same when it comes to your website.

The page title is seen at the top of the browser window when you visit a page. When you are creating a page, the first option that you have is to create the page title. So, make this your first step before proceeding to the next one. The titles of the pages also appear in search engine results. You will find the page title in the HTML file for your website. The text of the page title will be in between the "<title>" and "</title>" tags. You need to ensure that you make your page title very effective. Here's how you can do it:

- Formulate a sentence that incorporates all the keywords that you came up with earlier.

- Make sure that the title is no more than 70 characters in length. This is because no search engine has results with long page titles in them. If you make the title too long, you will be reducing the importance of the keywords in your title.

- Try to ensure that the keywords are at the beginning of the page title. They should be within the first few words in the sentence.

- Ensure that the title has a font that allows the viewers to read what you have written. Some of the best ones include Ariel and Georgia. Don't worry if your website does not use these; you can use them just for your SEO.

- Ensure that the name of your company is found at the end of the page title. But if you are a big brand, you can avoid this since most people will look for the pages on your website using your brand name.

- Try to ensure that you use a different title for each page. This will help you target the different keywords that you have listed.

Once you add the title, you will be given a permalink to the title. You can either choose the suggested permalink, or change it to your liking. This permalink is what will be the link to the page on your website.

THE META DESCRIPTION

Meta data is a feature that can help you attract many more visitors. These viewers will frequently view your website if you have meta data. It does not affect your ranking on a social network, but it is good to ensure that you have a few of your keywords mentioned in the meta description.

What is meta data? It is the text that is seen right below the link to your website provided by any search engine. This description is what will attract viewers to click the link to reach your website; however, this will only happen if there are keywords to be found in the meta description.

It is like reading the gist of what is to come. You have to try and condense it to tell the reader what is in store. It is similar to what is written below a headline in a newspaper to expand the idea of the headline.

You have to realize that the meta description is not found directly on your website; instead, it is just a summary of your website for search engines. If you do not include the meta description while coding the website, you will find that search engines just use information that is found on the page. This information is shown to viewers. The meta description is not understood well by most people and this is where you, as the owner of a business, may be making a mistake. So understand the difference and make the most of this feature. You will soon notice that your website will be much more discoverable, and that there is more scope for your website to show up higher on search engines.

THE HEADINGS

When you see a piece of text that appears larger than other text on the page, it is most probably a heading. This can be verified easily. You can view the HTML code of your website and check if the text comes between the tags <h1> and </h1>, <h2> and </h2>, or <h3> and </h3>. If you do not know how to do this, you can ask a developer to help you. In fact, it might be necessary for you to get professional help, as making a mistake can cause the headline to look bad.

The text in the headings is the part that is always read by search engines. Search engines assume that the text in the heading contains the keywords and it will ignore the rest of the text on the page. It is for this very reason that you will need to include keywords in the headings. It is best to use the <h1> tag, since that provides the largest font and has the most weight. There are other tags that you can use to enhance the view of your page, like <h4>, <h5>, <h6>, and <h7> tags. However, it is advisable not to use them since they do not have the same effect that the <h1>, <h2>, and the <h3> tags in your source code do. The other tags dilute the importance of the keywords that you use in them.

CASCADING STYLE SHEETS

Your website looks the way it does because of the code in your HTML. The HTML code is the back end to your website. It is the code that any search engine reads. The search engines extract the information that it finds relevant to a given search.

The cascading style sheet, or CSS, is what provides the layout of a given page in your website. This enables you to define how the headings and other elements in your page look. You have to use CSS for all your pages. However, you have to avoid using this information, which helps you enhance the layout of your page, in the HTML code of your page since your search engine may use that information.

IMAGES

When you were three years old, you loved the storybooks that had a lot of pictures included in them. This is the same when it comes to a website. Images always help in enhancing the experience of the users. You must also be well aware of the adage that a picture is worth a thousand words. The same applies to your website, where images will help you get noticed better. When you are working on the code of your website, you can try to use images that will describe your website. Again, if you are not aware of how to go about this, then make use of a developer. Make sure that you keep the following points in mind:

1. Do not use too many images on your page. This will make your page slow to load. This has a negative impact on viewers, since most of them are impatient, and will leave the website if it doesn't open fast enough. They won't want to wait for a page to load. They may choose to move to another page immediately.

2. When you have pictures on your page, try to insert text describing your pictures. Whether it is your product or a service, you need to describe it effectively. This is important since most search engines do not read images. They are generally only comfortable with reading text. Search engines may miss out on some important keywords if they are only found in the images, and not in the text. Try to separate the keywords using a hyphen or a dash (-).

THE DOMAIN INFO

You will find that websites that have been on the Internet for longer have a better ranking when compared to newer websites. This is because the length of time a domain is registered indicates the commitment of the owner. So when you start off, you must decide to stay with the same name and not change it from time to time. Try to remain loyal to the domain. Websites with short domain names may be considered spam.

THE GOOGLE CRAWL DATE

Google crawls through websites very often and updates the information that it displayes to viewers. The information that it updates is mostly keywords and other SEO information. You have to ensure that Google crawls through your website often. This can be done only if you produce new content on your website. If you have a blog, try posting stories on it on a regular basis, since that will help to ensure that Google crawls through the post. If you are busy, try collaborating with someone and ask them to add something as a guest post. Similarly, keep updating your website from time to time. Add something new like a product image or a description. All of this will ensure that Google crawls through your website.

AVOID KEYWORD STUFFING

You have read a lot about how important it is to ensure that you include keywords in your title, headings, and so on. You may believe that the more keywords you have the better your rank will be. You may begin filling your page up with all the keywords that you can think of. Please do not do that!

If you fill up your page with keywords, it may end up looking like a word salad and this will not interest visitors. This could also be viewed as a way of cheating search engines, which is bad thing to do. There are detectors that will ensure that you are not trying to trick search engines into believing that your page is good. If you are caught trying to trick them, search engines will usually leave your website out, leading to absolutely no publicity. The idea is to sprinkle keywords here and there and make it aesthetically pleasing. It should be like a well-peppered dish, which tastes much better than something full of pepper that is not mixed in well. So exercise caution and steer clear of using too many keywords in your description. It will end up being a big goof up!

COOKIES

Have you come across popups like the following when you are using the net?

"This website uses cookies to improve user experience. By using our website, you consent to our cookies in accordance with our cookie policy."

You can make use of these cookies in your business venture too. First, let us start with the basics. Let us learn about cookies.

A cookie is information that a site saves to your computer using your browser. There are millions who use the Internet every day. How can you keep track of all your consumers and frequent visitors? Cookies are the answer. Cookies tag individual computers so you'll know who is on your website. It is a non-invasive way to gather information about your visitors and their behavior. Obviously you will not be able to get all the information regarding your visitors. You can narrow down the preferences of your visitors and cater to that by delivering more personalized and targeted experience.

Cookie profiling or web profiling is having cookies provide basic information about your consumer's preferences. For example, if your website provides its contents in various languages, the visitor may select Spanish. If you used cookies, his language preference would have been stored in the cookie, resulting in faster and more convenient access by giving him the website in Spanish when he comes back. Basically, it creates a log of your visitors, stores their information, and applies the stored information the next time your website is accessed. The cookie file consists of the name of the server it was sent from, the lifetime of the cookie (if it is a persistent cookie) and a randomly generated number. This number becomes the visitor's computer's identity. So every time the visitor uses the computer to access your website, the server reads the number and remembers the visitor's preferences. If your website requires login, then these cookies will certainly help as it would have stored the username.

Cookies are of two types:

- Session cookies

- Persistent cookies.

Session cookies are temporary cookies that are created for temporary purposes and are active only for that particular session. When the visitor leaves the site, the cookie gets deleted. If you use such cookies, it treats everyone as a new visitor even though they have visited your website earlier.

Persistent cookies are also known as permanent cookies; the name speaks for itself. This type of cookie remains in the visitor's browser and gets re-activated when s/he comes back to your website. These cookies are the ones that remember your visitor's preferences. These permanent cookies also have expiry dates on them and they delete themselves once the expiry date arrives. When a regular visitor comes back, a new permanent cookie will be generated.

Imagine walking into your favorite restaurant and being greeted personally; the waitress already knows what you like, so she brings your usual order. How would you feel? Like you're at home? This is the same feeling that the visitors get when you use the cookies properly and give them a tailor-made experience. This will definitely keep your customers loyal and also bring in new visitors.

Of course you cannot depend on cookies fully, as many people do not like their online activity to be monitored and thus block or delete cookies.

CHAPTER FOUR

STEP 3 – CREATE A BLOG OR OTHER TYPE OF CONTENT

In the previous chapter, we looked at the second step of the process, which is understanding SEO and making use of keywords to help your website rise to the top of search engine results.

In this chapter, we will look at how you can start off on the Internet and build a steady audience base for yourself.

There are many platforms that have made it easy for a person to publish content on the Internet. You have been able to develop a good understanding of how important keywords are and how you can identify a list of those very words. You have also learnt how important it is to ensure that you optimize the content on your website for search engines.

The next step is to understand how you can ensure that more customers view your website. One way to make this happen is to begin blogging or posting content in different forms. How many times have you seen content about a website showing up on your Facebook account? I'm sure you have often visited a particular website after looking at the content. You could begin creating content for eBooks, and also by taking part in various conversations that happen on the Internet, such as on Twitter or Facebook. This will help you to make sure that as many people as possible are discovering your business and exploring it.

Blogging is the best solution, at least to start with, because not only is it easy, but it is effective too when it comes to reaching as many people as possible! Let us look at the things that you must bear in mind when you wish to start a blog.

How to Think About Different Business Strategies

When you are blogging, you need to stop thinking of yourself as the owner of a business, and start thinking of yourself as a publisher of a magazine. As a publisher, you have to publish articles that not only promote the business but also help in sharing information about the industry. This has to be done as it would be done in a regular industry.

You have to turn into your own public relations officer to ensure that people are seeing your stories the way you want them to.

You have to think about what you are writing about and the kind of words that you are using. You should never use terms, or jargon, that only people from your industry or the employees in your company would understand. Your aim is to publicize your company and you have to do whatever is in your power to show it in the best light. Don't take this step lightly, as it is your best chance at promoting your business effectively. When you were brainstorming for keywords, you thought about the different words your customers would use when they were describing your business. You will need to use those keywords in your blog posts, or any other posts that you are writing on your business. The second and third chapters of this book should have helped you understand the importance of the kind of words that you use.

SETTING UP WITH BLOGGING

It is important for you to gather content that your potential customers will find interesting. However, you will also need to find a way to put that content is online. There are many tools that will help you publish it online. Be sure that you select the perfect platform for blogging. You will need to keep the following things in mind:

1. The blog that you are starting should be part of your business's website. You need to realize that your website without a blog is like a regular brochure. A brochure never changes. You do not want your business website to look like that. They should have many connections and should be interlinked to each other.

2. Add new content to the blog on a regular basis. Search engines award higher rankings to those websites that have new content added consistently. You must update it from time to time and also have others contribute towards it. You will see how doing so will help your blog remain in the news and also increase your customer base. These higher rankings help you gain more consumers for your products and services.

It is important that your blogging software is easy to use. But it is even more important that the content that you create for your blog is interesting. Avoid making it monotonous. You will regret having wasted an opportunity where you could have used your power to increase your reach. There are quite a few blogging platforms that are easy to use and help you make your experience easier. These platforms have content management systems, which help you enter content with ease without having to worry about the coding. You will be able to edit information on the website without waiting for a developer to enter your content onto the page. If you are unable to find the ideal platform, then you must ask around and look for the best webhost for your blog. You can make use of Wordpress, as it is the world's number one content management system.

THE KEY COMPONENTS OF YOUR BLOG

As was mentioned earlier, it is important for you to study the different components of a topic if you wish to understand it thoroughly. In this segment, we will look at the key components of a blog.

There are many components that a blog must have and it is essential that you have this in order to gather more attention from your potential customers.

A TITLE THAT GRABS THE ATTENTION OF THE READER

It is your blog title that people will first lay their eyes on. You have to ensure that this title is the frosting on your cake. You have to use the correct keywords and make the title concise so that it grabs the attention of your readers. Only when it has the keywords that they are looking for will it pop up on their screen.

Try to keep it customer-oriented. That means that you must know your target audience in order to understand exactly what they like to read. It is like decoding their mindset and supplying them with something that will help them remain interested in what you are trying to say to them. It will help to do your research and ask people in your target age range about the keywords that they would look for in a blog.

TEXT THAT IS WELL–WRITTEN

Once you have got your title, you have to work on the content of your blog. Let us assume once again that you are in a bookstore. You have picked up a book with an interesting title and you begin reading. You read the first few pages and find that the book is very boring. In addition, the author does not come to the point even by the end of the book. Would you recommend such a book to a friend? It is the same when it comes to blogs. The article that you write must be precise and it must be formatted so that it is easy to read. You can break the content into different headings and paragraphs. More importantly, you have to write well and make sure that there are no errors. Keep it as interesting for your reader as possible, and don't fall into the trap of writing content that is not to your readers' taste. That will defeat the whole purpose of writing the blog and you will end up disappointed.

USE IMAGES AND VIDEOS

As mentioned in the previous chapter, it is always good to use images. There are times when they speak louder and more clearly than words. Let us assume that you are talking about an event where a thousand trees are planted in a dry patch of land. It is better if you have pictures to back up the text. It is even better to make sure that you follow up on that story and continue to show the growth of those plants. If you use images, you are breaking up the text into fragments, which makes the article more pleasing to the reader's eye. Similarly, you can make use of videos that are in keeping with your blog. Ideally, they should be professional photos that are clear and of good quality. This will make the blog more relatable and believable.

INCLUDE LINKS IN YOUR ARTICLE

When you are writing about something that has become famous all over the world, it is best to insert links. You are probably familiar with the term back-linking but, in case you are not, it refers to adding links to different sites in your blog. These links should all lead to different pages on your website. For example: If you are talking about a theory that has been developed recently, you cannot expect every person to be familiar with it. Therefore, it helps to insert a link to the content you are writing about. You can also insert links to your own website or to landing pages, which will help you gather more views to your content. This is discussed in detail in Chapter 6.

HAVE YOU DECIDED WHAT TO BLOG ABOUT?

If you have a business and have started a blog, it is for a reason. But what is this reason? Do you want educate the industry and your potential customers about your products? No? You will need to educate them on the happenings of the industry. You want them to learn about the problems that they, as potential customers, may face in the market. You must also tell them how your product helps them. Many people make the mistake of talking only about their products and its features, and fail to discuss why the product is a good fit for the customer. You must avoid making this mistake and touch on the topic. You have to tell them what benefits the product will give them and why they must choose it.

You can start blogging by answering ten basic questions that you think your customers may ask you. Then you can begin your blog by answering the most important question. You can make use of a FAQ system to ask and answer the various questions. However, you can only choose the questions if you put yourself in the shoes of your potential customers. Try to work on answering one question per week for the next ten weeks. This will help you create a great foundation for your blog and go a long way to ensure that your blog is successful.

Once you are done with answering these questions, you can work on different ways to make your blog interesting. For example:

- You can write about different products that the viewers may require and why they require these products.

- You can write about the happenings in your industry.

- You can write about changes that have been made to your products.

Make sure that you include images and that the content in your blog speaks volumes for your expertise. You do not want to have content that does not reflect your knowledge. Try to avoid making technical errors. Don't take your audience's intelligence for granted. If you provide them with redundant information, then it will be useless. You also have to show your potential customers that you are passionate about what you do. This can only be done when you write from your heart. But keep the business in the back of your mind when you are working on the content for your blog.

CHAPTER FIVE

STEP 4 – PROMOTING CONTENT AND PARTICIPATING IN DIFFERENT SOCIAL MEDIA

Social media has now become a great platform for setting up a business. Many marketers and businessmen use social media to establish and run their businesses. Marketers who leverage social media can distribute the products and services provided by their company with ease. They are able to increase their customer base to help grow their company significantly.

Social media is now one of the preferred ways to advertise websites. You instantly have millions of viewers who will be ready to purchase your products. But it is important to know how to reach these millions.

As a business owner, you should know that it is through social media that your existing and potential customers communicate among themselves and with you to better understand your products and services. This helps to ensure that the content on your website, and on other social media, passes on like wild fire. I'm sure you have heard of something going viral; however, this will only happen if you make use of the right sources to advertise your products and services. You have to choose the best sources and know where to place your product, in order to get the best results. Many new forms of social media are being introduced to the Internet. However, Facebook, LinkedIn, Twitter, and YouTube are the most famous ones. You will learn how to market on these platforms in the second part of this ebook.

How Do You Monitor Social Media?

It is important for you to leverage your business on social media. It is, however, more important to understand what is happening online when it comes to your line of business. You have to find the various conversations that are going on and identify the point at which you should respond to each conversation. Trying to get in just to look impressive will not cut it. You have to remain open to observing the conversation for a while before you give your opinion. Patience is a virtue and will pay off well if you showcase opinion and use it to your advantage. This section covers some of the most effective tools that you can use to monitor your business, and also to ensure that the industry mentions you on different social media.

Google Alerts

If you are a business owner, Google Alerts are your best friend. These alerts are like your alarms! You can set up multiple alerts on Google for your company. You can also set alarms to help you find articles to read or to understand what is happening in the industry that your business operates in. You can try to understand the way your products are affecting the market, as well. Set an alert that will notify you when there is a mention of your brand, or the products and services that you sell. If you don't know how to do this, ask someone to help you out. You will be required to link your email to the web in order to receive these alerts directly. Knowing how your website is faring will work as a big boost and help you do better. Since the alerts that you set for yourself are delivered to your inbox, you can access them from any connected device. You can ensure that you get these updates as frequently as you need or want. This is the best way in which you can track any mention of your brand, or products and services. You can also track the mention or use of any keywords on different parts of the web.

TWITTER

You can monitor the mentions of your brand name or products and services on Twitter using various tools like Twitter Search. You can also use CoTweet. This is a great tool that will help you manage multiple users on a Twitter account that is focused on the corporate aspect. You will be able to assign tweets to certain people in your company and ensure that they follow up on those tweets. The ways through which you can market your company on Twitter are the focus in the second part of this eBook.

FACEBOOK INSIGHTS

There are fan pages for most companies and brands on Facebook. You will need to stay abreast of things when you are branding and marketing your company. You will need to participate and begin discussions on your Facebook page. You can use your fan page to learn about various statistics. You can learn about the growth of your fan base and how many people have viewed your page. When you know this, you will be able to work on identifying ways by which you can improve the fan base or the views. This is also covered in detail in the second part of this eBook.

If you are serious about interacting with your audience and wish to answer to all their queries and keep them satisfied, then it is important that you employ someone who will take care of all your social media interactions. You have to give this person the liberty to say and do what they like as long as it is in your company's favor.

CHAPTER SIX

STEP 5 – CONVERT SITE TRAFFIC INTO THE LEADS FOR YOUR BUSINESS

You have now started your blog, and have also worked on optimizing the search for your website on the different search engines. You have started participating in various discussions that are held on social media, which will help you to promote your business.

If it has been a few weeks since you have done this, you should find an increase in the number of views that your website has had. This indicates that there is an increase in traffic to your company's website! But there is a potential problem that arises with this increase in traffic. That is, you may find that there has been no significant growth to your company. You may find that you are unable to generate new business. You know that there are people visiting your business website, but the people visiting are the same people who had come earlier. You are unable to gather any new views. So, although there are hundreds of people visiting you on a daily basis, you see that not many of them are buying anything or contributing to your site positively.

How can you gather more views? How can you ensure that there are new people who are viewing the content on your website? Well, let us find out!

The answer to this problem is quite simple. You need to focus on the rate of conversion. You have to work on converting the people who view your content into people who are buying from your business. You will need to create compelling orders to ensure that this happens. Consider this example. You are having a garage sale at home. You have an independent house in the farthest corner of the country and you only have a few friends who visit you frequently. They know that the products that you are selling are the best in their range, and they are able to afford those products with ease. However, you need to ensure that these friends go over to their friends and advertise your sale. This is what you must do for your business website, too!

All companies, small and big, rely on their current customers to bring in new ones. This ensures that they consistently have customers who will then bring in even more, so it is a loop that you have to create. But this is easier said than done. It is like you running a news site and finding new readers for your articles on a daily basis. This is only possible if the news site is putting out unique stories that are compelling for its current users to broadcast and to get others to read them.

Similarly, you can start providing compelling offers to your visitors. You could have a form that would require your visitors to fill in their details in order to take advantage of an offer that is being provided to them. Ensure that you do provide one person with the offer. You have to create a certain sense of intrigue in them and tell them something that they will want to share with their friends and family members. Lastly, you have to test and measure the entire process. You will also have to work on any changes that you will need to make. The steps below will help make it easier for you to work on conversion of your visitors.

STEP 1: DECIDE ON YOUR OFFER

This is the most important part of your campaign. For example, consider elections. When politicians are starting their campaigns, they will tell you all about what they will do to help you and the country as a whole. They talk about what they can offer you! You will choose the politician with the best offer.

You need to give your visitors an offer that they cannot refuse. I know it seems like a herculean task, since you will have a lot of customers who will belong to different categories. You have to try to cater to them as a whole, and aim at schemes that are designed to help their interest in you remain stable. So the offer should be unique to your site. This is because the offer is the initial attraction to your website. If the offer is one that they cannot take their eyes off of, you will be able to get them to fill out the form so you can collect their information. You have to ensure that the offer you make targets the sales that you intend on making. For example, if you are selling books on the Internet that will help a person improve their business communication skills, you will need to work on attracting the attention of executives who are looking for such workshops. For this, you can use whatever you can think of to attract the attention of your potential customers and sales managers! You can have webinars. You can also provide them with a free demo of your product if they wish for it!

STEP 2: CREATE CALLS TO ACTION

Once you have worked on the offer, you have to create compelling calls to actions or CTAs. The call to action is a link or a button that will enable the visitor to end up on a landing page. This page is where the user, or visitor, is asked to fill in a form that will provide a good amount of information about them. This information is gathered in order to provide them with the offer that they have signed up for.

After submitting the information, the visitor becomes a lead. Leads are the people whom your sales team can follow up with in order to convert them to sales leads. You can have a call to action button, a link, or even an HTML page but make certain that the link leads to the correct page. It is always good to have an effective call to action. You can use famous tag lines or even dialogue from movies that will help you make it effective. However, it is important to note that you should keep it as simple as possible for your visitors to remain interested in filling out the details. If you bombard them with several pages that take a long time to fill in, then you will end up chasing them away. Be precise and don't complicate it for them.

Step 3: Create Landing Pages

This is the final step for the offer. You will need to create landing pages right after you create the call to action.

When your visitors click on the call to action link or button, they are redirected to the landing page. This page will have the form that the visitors need to complete in order to receive or claim the offer that you are providing. There are many times when these calls to actions are not links. They may lead to a junk website or display an error. This may be a mistake on the part of the owner, but it is the lack of the link that will make your website less endearing to your potential customers and sales leads. These visitors may give up if they do not find a link to the landing page! You have to ensure that you check a million times to ensure that every call to action button on your website has a link attached to it!

The best way to check this issue is to test it out yourself. Ensure that the link is taking you to the desired page and not elsewhere. If it is taking you elsewhere, change it as soon as possible.

Landing pages are of two types:

Reference landing pages: These landing pages present information that is relevant to the visitor. Some reference landing pages include a summary of the products or services offered. The success of a particular reference landing page is often based on the revenue generated by any advertisements.

Transactional landing pages: These landing pages provide a form that needs to be filled out. They aim to encourage the visitor to share contact information. A technique used here is withholding certain information that will be made available only when contact information is provided. This way you gain a potential lead.

The landing page is where your visitors submit the information that will help them access your offer. You can also use the information that is collected on the forms. Your sales team will have to work on following up with the visitors. Once your visitor has completed the information on the form, it is a good idea to thank them. Therefore, you will need to insert a "thank you" page at the end of the entire process. You must design this page well and make the customers feel good about it. Incorporate cute pictures so that your customers are attracted to it.

STEP 4: YOU NEED TO TEST, MEASURE THE PROCESS, AND ALSO ITERATE

You have made your offer and created your call to action links and have also worked on the landing pages. But this is not where the process stops. You have to check how the entire process performs. You can try different offers or different call to action links and experiment. You will need to work on the landing pages and test different types. You have to decide on a particular process only after you have tried and tested different methods.

If you are short of time, you can hire someone to test it out for you. If none of your friends are up to it, you can hire freelancers to test it out. Whatever way you end up going, the fact of the matter remains that you have to have everything in great shape before going public with it, in order to gain as many customers as possible.

When a particular call to action has been on your page for a few months, you will need to change it. You can do this by changing the message that is being propagated through the call to action, or use a completely different one. You can then find out which of these calls to action performs better.

If you find that the landing page conversions are very low, you will have to work on the way the page looks. Try to ensure that the form is effective and to the point. Try different variations of the form. Once that is done, you can measure the results of those variations. Never be afraid to try new variations. You will have to dedicate some of your initial time and effort towards trying out what works, and what does not. You will know what works only if you try it out, as merely thinking something up will not cut it. You have to get down to doing it to see results. If you find that your first process was the best you can always swap back to that! It is always good to ensure that the process that you use has been tried and tested by you. This will ensure that the process is foolproof. You will also be able to gather more views and leads!

CHAPTER SEVEN

STEP 6- USE LEADS IN YOUR EMAILS WHEN MARKETING

Many surveys have been conducted on online marketing. The results of these surveys show that close to 70 percent of leads buy something. They may buy the commodities or services from your competitors, too! But they are clever enough to not do it right away.

The companies that build a good relationship with their leads are those that have great success in turning their leads into potential buyers and customers. Consider this example: Flipkart had initially started out by selling books. The website began to function at a time when ecommerce was picking up. If people purchased books from Flipkart they were considered to be gods. Through brilliant marketing, Flipkart sold a good amount of books in the first run and has now expanded into selling a wide range of products. This is because they are able to keep track of all their customers and keep in touch with them. They send them emails and messages to help them know what offers are the best for them. This is because the sales team at Flipkart is nurturing the leads that it obtains. If you notice carefully, they have slowly made the transition through some strategies that have worked in their favor. They did not jump the gun and go all in with different products right from the beginning. They wisely waited for their leads to convert to regular customers and then capitalized on it. Now let us see how you can do the same.

What is lead nurturing? It is the process by which a business owner develops a relationship with potential customers. They obtain the information on these potential customers through the forms that they leave on the landing pages. The business owner (you) must work on sending relevant and valuable messages to your leads in a timely manner. These messages should contain information that benefits the lead and the company! The final goal of this process is to ensure that your leads choose your company over any other company out there! They have to WANT to do business with you! In other words, it is all about building a rapport with your customers. You will see that it helps your company in leaps and bounds.

THE BEST PRACTICES OF EMAIL MARKETING

This section covers the best ways through which you can ensure that you are able to market your company and the offers that you provide. You can follow the steps below to provide your viewers the best experience possible.

Opt-Ins

Opt-in email is usually used to bring in new visitors who can potentially turn into customers. When a visitor is on your transactional landing page, you gather information about the person and get some contact information. This process where information is being transacted is called an opt-in.

Opt-ins are of two types:

1. Unconfirmed opt-in/single opt-in

2. Confirmed opt-in/ double opt-in

In single opt-in, the visitor first provides an email that is left unverified. This email address may contain spelling mistakes and, when you actually send an email to the address, it will end up in spam as junk mail. So, to make sure that you are getting the correct information, make use of a double opt-in method, in which you send a confirmation mail to the address and ask them to click on the link that you have provided in the mail to make sure you are reaching the correct person. Here there is a twofold opt-in because the first opt-in is when they enter their email address in your landing page and the second is when they click on the special web link sent in their verification mail. This also brings you customers who are actually interested in your product. There may be a few people who had accidentally opted in but, if they do not verify the email address, then you'll know that the visitor wasn't actually interested in your product so you can stop wooing them.

If you do use the single opt-in method, the one major advantage is that your mailing list will probably grow faster because there are a lot of apparent subscriptions for your product. The disadvantages of opting for this method are that your list quality is diminished. You will not reach customers who actually need your products and you will be wasting your time sending mails to somebody's spam box. Going for double opt-ins sure does increase the quality of your list and your customers, but one major disadvantage is that 20% of the genuine customers will not complete the process because they will forget to click the link or the mail will end up in their spam box because of filters.

When you do finally send your newsletter or marketing communications, always include the opportunity to unsubscribe. Another option to have in marketing mails is "update subscription preferences." You can use this to filter customers who will actually buy your product.

BUILDING THE LIST OF LEADS

This is an extremely important part of your marketing strategy. In the previous chapter, you learnt about landing pages. The landing page is where you provide your visitors with a form that will help them avail your offer:

- When you create a form, ensure that there is an opt–in option. You need to ask them for their email addresses in order to communicate with them. This allows your viewers, or visitors, to choose to receive messages from you.

- You have to give your visitors a compelling reason to opt in. It could be for your ebook or even a newsletter. Why should they choose your newsletter? How is it better than the other newsletters that are available in the market? Is there certain information that is unique to your newsletter? You will need to word the benefits very explicitly to enable your customers to understand it and readily accept it.

-Do you want to send messages to every person who is on your list? That is honestly a waste of time. It is always good to send messages to those people who have opted to receive messages from you. You can follow the principle of Seth Godin. He believed that a business owner must send a message to a person or a potential customer, only if he will be upset about not having received the message from the business owner. It is as simple as that and straight to the point. You don't want to go after people who are not your ideal leads, and look for those that are really interested in you and your products.

SENDING MESSAGES

This is an extremely important aspect that you need to consider. You cannot expect immediate results if you do not send the right messages. This section helps you identify the different aspects to consider when you are sending messages:

- You have to stay relevant. You have to keep a track of what interested your visitor, or your potential lead. Was it a particular ebook? Was it an article on a trending topic? You have to make a list of what your leads view, too! Send them only emails or messages with information on what they are looking for. This you will know from looking at their personal information. That is exactly why you should get them to provide you with the correct information.

- When you send emails, try to get personal with your leads. You will have to use your name and your email address. This will give them the idea that you are available for them to contact you whenever they need something. Try to personalize the message. You have to add their name and directly address them. Make sure that you let them know why you are sending this email. You can begin the email with "Hey, we noticed that you have shown keen interest in this particular article … This may interest you too!"

-You have to make sure that the message you share with your viewers adds value to them. You will need to step into the shoes of your viewers and ask yourself this question: "What is in it for me?" You will have to ensure that you are not sending them an email or a message just to market your product. You have to ensure that they understand that you are sending them a message since you believe that the product or service you are offering offers value to them! You have to make them they believe that! Again, don't take your consumers' intelligence for granted. That will be a big mistake.

-Never rely entirely on the images that you attach to the messages. There are a lot of email clients that do not allow images to load in their browsers automatically. If you only use an image as the email, there are times that it will backfire on you. Your viewers may not be able to load the images in their browsers. You can use the image as a supplement, or use it to enhance the content that you are using in your email. You have to ensure that you have enough text in your email before you send it to your potential clients. If you are keen on using images, try to keep them as simple as possible. A busy email can be quite confusing and your client might not be able to identify the main topic in it.

- You need to maintain consistency. You need to ensure that your leads are waiting for your emails and messages. You have to stick to what you get them used to. If you begin by sending emails to them daily, weekly, or even monthly, you need to stick to it! If you do deviate from your schedule, inform your leads why. It is important that they do not feel left out. They might mail you back asking about it and that is not an ideal situation. Don't give them that chance and keep them updated at all times. Make sure that the reason you are giving them is valid!

- Try to ensure that you do not let the law bring you down! You will need to keep track of all the regulations that have been laid out to ensure that there is minimal spam when you are sending emails. You should go through the CAN-SPAM regulations to keep yourself updated!

Converting Your Visitors into Leads

You may wonder what you have to do here. You have a major role to play. When a person opens your email or message, you have to explicitly state what you need them to do! Do you want them to click on a link? Do you need them to read an article? You have to spell it out for them and tell them exactly you want them to do for you.

You will need to include a call to action link or a button that will lead your visitors to a landing page where they will perform the action that you want them to do. You can convert this visitor into another lead and ensure that they want to do business with you.

The landing page in your email is a part of the campaign. That is the tool that you are using to lure these leads that you wish to convert into your customers. You need to remember that, when you are marketing using email and messages, it does not stop with just a click. You will need to have a landing page where the conversion takes place. You have to ensure that your email and the landing page are in a proper flow. The previous chapter will help you identify how to make sure that this flow is maintained!

MEASURING THE CONVERSIONS

This is the last part to your flow of email marketing! You can use the following methods to measure the conversion:

- The best way to measure your responses is the click-through rate (CTR). When you send an email to people, how do you count the number of people who have clicked on the link that leads to your landing page? Through the CTR, you will be able to understand how compelling your message and offers are. You will then be able to experiment with different subject lines and also work on the calls to action links. You will also be able to work on the timing of your emails. All of these are important and only a perfect strategy will help you attain the desired results.

- Another method for measuring the conversion is the open rate. This count the number of visitors or leads who took the time to open the image that you sent in your email. This is an unreliable measure, since there are clients who do not open the images that are sent in the email. The open rate uses the images as a measure of counting. You can focus on the number of times your email has been opened.

- You have to make sure that you remove yourself from any levels of spam or annoyance. There are times when people will want to unsubscribe from receiving your emails. This count should not exceed 5%. If you find that the rate has begun to increase, check your lists. Make sure that you do not send emails or messages to people who have not subscribed for your regular updates.

- The final step is to measure the rate of conversion. When you send out emails, you should make note of the number of people who have bothered to check your landing page and reconvert as users.

When you are nurturing your leads, you should also be developing relationships with them. You have to keep in mind that you should not limit your communication just to emails or messages. You will have to learn how to communicate with them through social media. This is covered in detail in the second part of this ebook.

Distribution Lists

A distribution lists is an email feature that allows you to send an email message to a collective group of people at the same time in one go. Instead of typing out each and every email address that you've collected through social media in the address bar and then sending the messages one by one, you can easily club them together under one list and send the email just once. This whole group is addressed as one single recipient.

DISTRIBUTION LIST IN MICROSOFT EXCHANGE:

Step 1: On the File menu, point to "New," and then click "Distribution List".

Step 2:   In the Name box, type the name of your distribution list. (For example, "Political Friends.")

Step 3:   On the Distribution List tab, click "Select Members."

Step 4:   In the Address Book drop-down list, click the address book that contains the email addresses you want to include in your distribution list.

Step 5:   In the Search box, type a name that you want to include. When the name you're searching for appears in the list below, click it, and then click "Members."

Step 6:   Do this for each person whom you want to add to the distribution list, and then click "OK."

DISTRIBUTION LIST IN GMAIL:

Step 1: Click Contacts under the Gmail menu.

The Google Contact Manager is divided into two parts:

1. The left section shows your existing groups and functions. Some groups are automatically created based on your activities.

2. The right section displays the contact's name and email addresses.

Step 2: In this scenario, you scroll the list of contacts and check the ones you wish to include. Once you check a contact, the Groups button appears.

Step 3: Click the Groups button and select "Create new."

Step 4: Give your group a distinctive name and click "OK."

Your new group should show on the left side, with an indicator of how many contacts are in this group.

DISTRIBUTION LIST IN YAHOO

Step 1: Click on the *Contacts* tab on the top.

Step 2: Click the plus ("+") sign to add a new list.

Step 3: Type in the desired name for the new list.

Step 4: Select all of the contacts you want to add to your list.

Step 5: Click "Assign to Lists."

Step 6: Click the list you want to add the contacts to and then click "Done."

DISTRIBUTION LIST IN OUTLOOK

Step 1: Click dropdown menu in top left corner.

Step 2: Click *People* option.

Step 3: Click dropdown menu on the top by "New."

Step 4: Click "New group."

Step 5: Click *Group name* and *Add members* and then click "Save" on the bottom when you're finished adding all members.

DISTRIBUTION LIST IN AOL

Step 1: Click the *Contacts* tab on the left side.

Step 2: Click *New List* on top of page under the search bar.

Step 3: Type in the desired name for the list. Add contacts to the list and, when done, click "Add List."

DISTRIBUTION LIST IN MAC MAIL

Step 1: Open up the app "Contacts" or "Address Book".

Step 2: Click *File* on the top of the screen and then click *New Group*.

Step 3: Type in the desired "Group name" and click *Enter*.

Step 4: To add contacts to your group, go to "All Contacts" and highlight all contacts you wish to add, then drag them to the desired group.

CHAPTER EIGHT

STEP 7- ENSURE THAT YOU ARE MOBILE FRIENDLY

These days you find every person, whether young or old, flaunting a new mobile phone that they have purchased, most likely from an online site. Everyone wants to be ahead when it comes to technology. This is a bonus to the people who want to use the social media as their means for marketing. Verizon conducted a survey showing that over 13 million iPhones were sold in the year 2011 alone.

If you are willing to market through the Internet that is used on mobile phones, you need to consider the idea of creating entertainment. You will have to create quality content through entertainment. For example, consider the Australian Metro. They wanted to tell people about how to stay safe on their trains. They created a video called "Dumb Ways to Die." This video is hilarious and entertaining but it helps establish the importance of staying safe in train stations. You will need to come up with innovative ideas to get people to view your advertisements on their mobile phones.

OPTIMIZING CONTENT FOR MOBILE PHONES

Mobile marketing is a term that is being thrown around in many marketing circles. But this is where most people are wrong. They are implying different meanings when they say mobile marketing. There may be many meanings to mobile marketing, but the primary meaning is that the business owner wants to convey a message to viewers through a mobile phone.

You will need to develop an application that is compatible with mobile phones. It is not the same as what you would create for your website. There are many differences that you need to know about to in order to create something that is easy to see on a phone. When you are designing an application for mobile phones, you will need to ensure that it is relevant to your business. You have to make enough content to support a mobile application. It is always good to begin with SEO and email marketing before you jump into marketing through phones. If you are in a business that is beginning to use a mobile application to market your business, you will need to see to it that your website design is easy to navigate when it is viewed on a phone.

WHAT TO WORRY ABOUT WHEN MARKETING THROUGH MOBILE PHONES

There are certain things that will need to be taken care of when you are marketing through mobile phones. This section covers those worrisome things.

CALLS TO ACTION AND EMAILS

When you use a website to market your company and its products and services, you do not have to worry about the calls to action. You do not have to worry about the size of the files or even about the landing pages when you are only working on

Internet marketing. But when it comes to mobile devices, you have to worry about the way in which the content is viewed on the phone. You will need to worry about the accessibility of the content on your website. It is also important to think about how the calls to action and the emails will work on the mobile devices.

DOWNLOADS

When you send the viewers an email or a message with the calls to action, you need to include the landing pages. But when it comes to the mobile phone, you also have to worry about how the file or form will appear on the phone screen. If you are asking the people to download the form, you will have to see how it will look on a mobile phone.

VIDEO

In 2011, it was stated by Video Bytemobile that close to 60 percent of the traffic on different smartphones was for videos only. It also stated that the user accounts that mobile phone users use close to 90 percent of mobile network traffic. This shows that a very small number of mobile phone users consume much of the mobile bandwidth.

The data mentioned above highlights some of the most critical aspects of the evolution of the mobile web. It has been seen that the cost of consumption for mobile bandwidth will rise. It is essential that the marketers begin to develop websites that do not consume too much mobile bandwidth. You should not expect your consumers to stream videos with large bandwidth demands. You have to try to provide a very short summary of the video right below the video for the consumers using cellular network connections. If these users are connected to Wi-Fi at their homes or anywhere else, you can give them the option to download the video.

CHAPTER NINE

STEP 8- ANALYSIS AND REFINEMENT OF STRATEGIES

This is a very important step that every marketer must take. You have to provide your customers with the best service possible. This can be done only if you adopt marketing methods that are sound and allow you to connect with consumers on a large scale. Amazon and Flipkart are the most popular ecommerce websites. This is because they have marketed their brand names in a brilliant way. They have advertisements that cater to different segments of society. They start newer advertisements if they find that the older advertisements have not had the desired effect on the market. This is because they analyze and refine their marketing strategies frequently.

ROI – Revenue on Investment

Maybe you follow all the advice given in this book. You spend so much time on social media putting every bit of advice you've heard into action to market via social media. You've spent hard-earned money on making your product available online, and spent it on ads. You have spent many days trying to come up with unique strategies to make your website better than others and trying to find out what your unique selling point is. If it were a different type of business, you expect returns on your investment and that should not change here. You have invested in your business and you need to see if your efforts have paid off and that can be done by measuring your ROI. Measuring revenue on investment is hard because the algorithms used in this process keep changing, so there are a few steps for you to measure your ROI.

First, you need to set goals. Determine what scales you are going to use to determine your success. It can be leads or clicks or new email addresses in your mailing list. Other metrics are reach, conversion rate, traffic, online purchases, social interactions, link clicks, etc.

You then need to find out which social media you are going to choose. Find where your audience spends their time. Maybe you have marketed on all the major platforms, so it is hard because there is activity on all the sites. Then choose the one site where you spent a lot of investment in marketing and keep that as your data point.

Then make a list of all the money that was spent on that social media site. Track down the time spent in the marketing, cost of all ads related to that site, and other activities that made up the marketing efforts in that platform.

Put down the findings in an organized manner. You can put it down in a timeframe to make it easier – weekly, monthly, quarterly, yearly, etc.

Now that you have your results, review them. Find out what worked for you and what didn't and then reset your goals and make the concerned changes.

It can be hard to measure ROI because you might not know when to measure. The investment that you make now will pay off maybe in another year or even next week. The trends of social media are hard to solidify. The influence varies. It is also hard to put a value on intangible things like loyalty and sentiments. Many researchers have found out that, rather than revenue being generated by social media marketing, only brand presence and awareness have increased. Many people might not trust online shopping and would rather go the old traditional way of face-to-face shopping. Thus the effect of marketing in social media is not set in stone. But many people will follow your product diligently online and make up for potential customers. So many factors play into social marketing, making the measurement of ROI very difficult. Nonetheless, it should not stop you from taking stock of what you have achieved and what you can change to achieve more.

THE FIVE STEPS TO ANALYZE AND REFINE STRATEGIES

This section covers the five basic steps that you as a business owner can implement to analyze your marketing strategies.

INCORPORATE AN ANALYTICS PROGRAM

You will need to constantly monitor the technology that you use as well as your marketing strategies using the technology. This is difficult since it has to be done on a regular basis. You can make life easier for you by using analytics software. Various software programs can be used to analyze the traffic to your website, conversion rates, and much more.

IDENTIFY WHAT IT IS THAT YOU WANT TO CHANGE

There are many things that you may have to change. Instead of jumping in and making changes to everything, you should decide what you want to target first. Assume that you have to work on the titles, the content, and the images on your page. You cannot work on all of these at once. You will have to work on it step by step. Start working on the title, since that is the most important part of your page. You can then move on to analyzing the content and then the images. Try to follow a systematic process.

Once you have done that, can ask yourself the following questions.

1. Do you want more traffic for your website?

2. Do you want to convert the visitors into leads?

You also have to try looking for different ways in which you will be able to create new avenues for yourself. Initially Flipkart only sold books but, when it became a hit with consumers, Flipkart began to expand into other departments. You now have numerous departments from which you can buy what you want most.

IDENTIFY METRICS FOR YOUR SUCCESS

You have to have a quantifiable means of measuring success. You should avoid having a system that only gives you dichotomous answers. For example, try to state that your new venture would be a success if there were 10,000 views in a day.

WORK ON REFINING YOUR STRATEGIES

You have worked on the various parts of your strategy. You have also decided that there are things that you will have to work on. You have to analyze where your programs or marketing strategies have performed and where they have not. Once you do this, you will be able to modify what does not work and try to see if you can enhance the programs that are working.

EVALUATE YOUR STRATEGIES

You have made changes to your strategies and have begun to use them. Start measuring your success using the metric that you have decided on. If you find that you are able to meet the metric that you have set, you can continue with the same strategy. You will have to work on doing things differently otherwise. You will need to monitor the changes made continuously in order to have an effect that lasts for the long term!

THE METRICS TO ANALYZE SUCCESS

You have been asked to identify a metric that will help you measure your success. You have also been told that the metric needs to be quantifiable. But what sort of metrics can you use?

In order to ensure that the changes you make to your strategies have a good impact, you have to monitor a lot of aspects. For this, it is best if you install or use analytics software. You will need to define a set of metrics that can be measured by the analytics software too! This section covers a few of the metrics that you can use to make sure that your website is working fine.

THE GRADE OF YOUR WEBSITE

This is the best metric of all! This tells you how well you have optimized your website. You can do this using an online tool called the Website Grader, which gives you monthly updates on how well you are doing with respect to the grading of your website.

TRAFFIC

The traffic is a measure of the number of people who are visiting your website regularly. This is a good metric to keep track of since you will know the effect that the changes you make to your website have on your potential consumers.

LEADS

This is an extremely important measure for any business owner. When you are working on strategies for your company, you always want to ensure that the viewers become potential customers, and in turn lead other customers to you. You have to keep track of how many people make the effort to proceed to the landing page to avail themselves of your offers.

CUSTOMERS

How many sales have you made this month? People have visited your website. But how many of those people have taken you up on your offers or the products and services that you sell? This number is of great importance.

THE COST OF ACQUIRING NEW CUSTOMERS

You have to make new changes to your website, or you may have to take the extra effort to approach new customers. There is a cost that you will incur when you do this. You have to keep track of those costs as well!

HOW MANY NEW VISITORS?

You may have a good amount of traffic. But how many people return to your website? How many of the people coming to your website are new customers? It is good to have visitors coming back. But it is also important to attract new customers. This means that there are people who have been looking out for your website. If you have people who are returning to your website, you need to feel good about that, too. This means that you have a website that has something to return to. You have to try to find a balance between the two.

Once you have done all these you are ready to go to the next part of the book! You will now be able to use social media to help you market your products and services! It will take time for you to get the hang of it, but do not fret. You will be able to ensure that your company has a good brand image in no time.

PART TWO

SOCIAL MEDIA MARKETING

CHAPTER TEN

STEPS FOR IMPROVING THE CONTENT

Before we begin to understand what goes into marketing content on different social media, let us brush up on the main aspects that we need to keep in mind when writing content for the products and services that your company has to offer.

This chapter covers some of the simplest aspects that you will need to cover in order to ensure that you have reached all the broad goals that you have set for yourself.

KEYWORDS

This should be your mantra! You have to always work on the keywords that you are using in your text. You have to make sure that the keywords you use vary. Try coming up with a good list of keywords that show variations. This will ensure that you are found on the search engines. You can also try to use different keywords on different pages on your website. You can do this in a million different ways!

ON–PAGE SEO

This is a very important thing to do. It is also extremely simple to do. The first part of this book covers the basic rules that you have to follow in order to work on the on–page SEO. These changes will help in boosting the visits to your page. If you want to test it, try to change a certain aspect of your website, maybe the title or the heading. You may find an increase in the traffic.

CONVERSIONS

You have been told about the importance of conversions! Now you have to try to find new ways through which you can see that your visitors have become your consumers and have led you to other consumers. You can try to do this by making the conversion form look more prominent on the page. Or you can publicize the conversion form on various social media that are listed below.

CONTENT STRATEGY

The content plays a major role in attracting the attention of the visitors. It is like a book review. When you pick up a book, you want to know what the story entails. If the summary at the back of the book does not interest you, you will not purchase the book. The book could be a bestseller for all you care. The same goes for the content on the website. It is only through the content that you will be able to generate more traffic. This would imply that you have the opportunity to focus on the business, but also focus on the kind of content that you are looking to deliver.

USE SOCIAL MEDIA FOR PROMOTIONS

As mentioned above, you can use social media to publicize your conversion forms. You could also use social media to help you attract more visitors. This part of the book helps you understand the workings of four of the most happening social media—Facebook, Twitter, LinkedIn, and YouTube. You must always work on improving the look of your website on these platforms.

NURTURING YOUR LEADS

This is an extremely important aspect that you will need to consider. You have to keep a close eye on your leads. The communication you have with your leads must not be haphazard. You should not send them too many or too few emails. Make sure that the content in your email is also appropriate for the audience. You have to ensure you experiment with the content on a regular basis!

Now that you have brushed up on all the main aspects of social media marketing, you are ready to learn how you should market on social media platforms!

CHAPTER ELEVEN

DOMINATE FACEBOOK MARKETING

If you own a small business, you have probably been told you "should" be using Facebook to promote your business or products by everyone you know. With almost a billion and half active users, at least several thousand should take an interest in what you do.

HOW TO USE FACEBOOK FOR SMALL BUSINESS MARKETING

Making a page for your business or products and getting a few likes from some friends and family members will not do your business much good, though; learning how to master Facebook marketing, on the other hand, will allow you to attract visitors and to convert them into fans and eventually into customers.

This chapter of the ebook will guide you through how to harness the full potential of social media by teaching you how to set up, optimize, and monetize your business's Facebook page. But before that, you will need to know what the benefits of using Facebook for business marketing are.

BENEFITS OF USING FACEBOOK FOR BUSINESS MARKETING

There are some people who believe that Facebook is dead! This is totally untrue! There are many benefits to using Facebook for marketing your business! It is essential that you remember these before you get into marketing your business through Facebook.

EXPOSURE TO POTENTIAL CUSTOMERS

There are close to 1.19 billion users on Facebook! Does this answer the question? You will be able to reach out to that many people by placing one advertisement on Facebook. You may not be able to reach out to all of them, but there may be one person who will lead your business to a hundred other people! You yourself must have many friends, and then they have their friends, and those have theirs, etc. Add them all up and you are sure to have hundreds of people all looking at your ads. Isn't that enough to at least get a head start in this field?

OBTAIN MORE LEADS

This is one thing that you will never have to worry about on Facebook. You will find a lot of people who like your page and also keep a constant look out for your posts. But what would you do if Facebook disappeared one day? No, don't panic, that's just a thought and hope that day never comes. You would be unable to keep in touch with your customers. You have to ensure that you maintain a good rapport with all the people who have liked your page. This is the only way you can ensure that you have a good number of leads.

LOW MARKETING EXPENSES

One big headache that most new business owners need to deal with is the marketing cost of their products. They fear that these costs will end up being so big that they will eat into their profits. But, with Facebook, you do not have to pay anyone to take pictures for you to post on your page. You can do that yourself. You may own a confectionary store. You do not need to hire a professional photographer to take pictures of the items that you are selling. You can do that on your own! You can take the pictures and post them on your page. I'm sure you have seen pictures put up by many companies and realized that they have a personal touch to them. You can do the same.

YOU CAN REACH A TARGET AUDIENCE

Just because there are close to 1.19 billion users on Facebook, you cannot expect that all of them will like your page. In fact, you do not want all of them to like your page. This is because only a few of them will want to participate in the discussions that you hold in your group. You will be able to track the required audience if you take some time to look for them. There will be people who have liked pages that are relevant to the content that you have put up. Target those people! Keep in touch with them.

YOU HAVE FACEBOOK INSIGHTS

This is your best friend! This helps you quantify all you need to know! You are able to view the number of people who like your page, the number of pages you like, the way you have engaged with the people on your page and so on. You can also see how well you performed over the last year!

YOU WILL BE ABLE TO BUILD BRAND LOYALTY

This is a big thing for any business owner. You always strive to ensure that your customers stay loyal to you and you stay loyal to your customers. How can you do this on Facebook? All you need to do is continue to provide your viewers with the right content.

You can rest assured that they will continue following you and reading every post that you put up.

STEP 1: CREATE A FACEBOOK PAGE FOR YOUR BUSINESS

If you are regular Facebook user, you are probably familiar with the features of a personal account, but know very little about the amazing marketing features that Facebook has to offer. Unlike an individual Facebook profile that requires other users to "friend" you and you to decline or accept friend requests, a Facebook page requires individual users and other pages to "like" it. This allows them to follow and interact with the page but keep their information private. Unlike friend connections, Facebook pages' connections are one-way.

Once you have created a Facebook page, you can grant people access to edit the page, post updates, or like the page. You can also track the page's activity to see which posts generate a buzz and which ones do not in the Insights section. The page offers several tools that the page owner can use to build an audience, create simple ads, and interact with your fans.

STEP 2: SET UP YOUR PAGE

Once your page has been created, take some time to customize it, applying the same branding that your website uses, if you have one. You can do this by:

1. Uploading an eye-catching cover photo that will appear on top of the Facebook page.

2. Using your business's logo as the page's profile picture. Note that the profile picture is the image that will be attached to all the page's posts.

3. Providing detailed information about the business in the about section of the page. This can include a brief history of the business, its mission or description, location and contact information including a phone number, and a link to your business's official website.

Remember to make use of photographs that you have taken yourself. That will make you look genuine. For example, if you are a bakery owner, you must neatly arrange all your products and showcase them on your page. You can add in a few fun elements and make it interesting. You must also provide the user with in-depth insight into what you have on offer for them at the bakery. It will pay to mention all the ingredients that you use and where you acquire them. All these small details will help them connect with you and transparency will pay off well. You must also clearly mention your address so that people know where to reach you. Check all these small points before going live with your page to eliminate discrepancies. Maintain a separate telephone for your business and advertise it so that people can reach you directly.

At this stage, your Facebook page will be functional and you can start using it right away. However, you can enhance it further by adding Facebook ads that boost the page's performance and even appearance.

STEP 3: BUILD A FOLLOWING

Once you set up your Facebook page, you can invite your friends and existing contacts to like the page. The page will have a handy "Build Audience" tab that you can use to get the initial likes you need to get started. Be sure to make the page interesting by publishing a post or two before you start inviting people; users are often skeptical of pages that have not shared anything.

Remember that, when someone likes your Facebook page, their friends and at times even friends of friends (depending on their privacy settings) can see it; it will be in your best interest to attract the attention of those people too.

There are many ways to build a Facebook page fan base. The easiest and most effective way, though, is to constantly create content and share it in a way that it reaches the widest audience.

Use the following straightforward rules to increase the number of people who like your page by simply mastering the art of online seduction through creative and ethical content sharing.

1. Use hashtags in your posts to make them discoverable, e.g., #Marathon. Because your page's posts are public, people can find them when they click such a hashtag posted by anyone on Facebook, even posts shared by other users. However, do not overuse hashtags on Facebook, as they can be distracting. You cannot use a hashtag on every post unlike on Twitter posts.

2. Get more exposure by liking other pages and interacting with their posts. Find local businesses and pages that share content relevant to your industry and like them, but do not ask them to like you back, at least not directly.

3. Do you have an active business blog? Whenever you publish a post, share it on Facebook and briefly explain why it would be a good read. Keep the page

alive by announcing upcoming events and posting any special offers and discounts your business is offering, and encourage users to interact by posing questions and sharing posts and updates by other pages.

4. Now and then, make your posts focus on the user. You can do this by sharing content that is not promotional in nature, e.g., inspirational quotes, funny memes, viral videos, and fast response questions.

On your website, encourage your fans to ask questions or raise any business, product, or service concerns on Facebook. Be sure to respond to any criticism, complaint, or concern that users raise on comment sections of your posts or inbox messages professionally and positively.

While you have the freedom to choose what to share, there are types of content you must never share. These include copyrighted content and images, spam and spam-like contents, controversial topics, and "business-as-usual" content when there is a national tragedy.

STEP 4: PROMOTE YOUR PAGE

Facebook pages make it very easy to get into paid Facebook promotions that start from under $10 a day. Facebook ads are very simple—there are templates to use under "Build Your Audience" when you click on *Promote Your Page*. All it takes is selecting an image to upload, coming up with a one-line title, and choosing the profiles of your target audience based on location and up to ten other interests.

You can also promote your page by boosting a specific post. A "Boost" would make the post or status update appear in the Home feed of targeted users as a "Suggested Post." All the step-by-step instructions on how to achieve this appear when you click on the *Boost* button at the bottom of every published post.

When you promote a page or a post, you can choose to run the ad campaign for a day, within your budget, continuously, or anything in between. This is a very useful feature that can automate your page and keep it active and engaging.

STEP 5: MEASURE AND ANALYZE WHAT'S WORKING AND WHAT IS NOT

The best thing about using Facebook as a marketing tool is that you can use inbuilt tools to measure and evaluate performance and to decide what is working and what is not. If you already have clear social media marketing goals, you can consistently measure the marketing campaign's performance and adjust accordingly.

Facebook has a dynamic audience and activity metrics system that can show you which areas of your marketing approach need improvement, and click-through statistics that show how much traffic converts to sign-ups. Be sure that you monitor engagement and integrate your social media campaign with other marketing channels, because having a Facebook page is not sufficient to drive sales through the roof.

As an agile marketing channel, Facebook is a dominant social platform that small business entrepreneurs can use with ease to boost their brand awareness, sales and exposure to potential and existing clients. Therefore, you should manage your business Facebook page in an agile manner by:

1. Starting small

2. Constantly measuring and monitoring

3. Adjusting your strategy accordingly

4. Growing consistently.

CHAPTER TWELVE

DOMINATE TWITTER MARKETING

If you have a business and have not created a business Twitter account, that should be the next item on your to-do list. Twitter is a powerful networking and marketing tool that you can use to gain followers (read: customers), engage with them, and generate more sales leads.

WHAT IS TWITTER?

Twitter is a microblogging platform you can use to create short 140-character text posts to share publicly, along with other media content, with the people that follow you. The posts use hashtags to make them findable on searches.

Twitter is not a tool that you can post free ads on. While you can use it to promote your business and products, blatant advertising such as spamming will never help your business. Having a business Twitter handle is not synonymous with having a social media strategy, it simply means you are ready to make use of the immensely beneficial tools that the platform makes available for those that learn to use it.

To use Twitter as a social marketing tool and make the 140-character tweets work for your business, you must be Twitter-savvy. Follow these simple steps to master the art of Twitter social marketing and dominate Twitter marketing. Before you do this, you will need to analyze the reasons behind using Twitter as a means of marketing.

BENEFITS OF USING TWITTER FOR BUSINESS MARKETING

Twitter helps you communicate with your customers, either current or potential, through your account. You can create your account if you are willing to do this! There are various benefits of using Twitter to market your business. You can use Twitter and also ensure that you are complementing it with other channels of communication.

COMMUNICATING

On Twitter, you can see to it that your followers have current information about your business. They know about every update that occurs. If you cannot picture this, you can use a footballer's account as an example. They update their followers on what is happening in their lives. Their followers would know when they had a baby, or what they are planning to name their baby even before it is out in the news. You will also be able to communicate with your followers. You can try to establish a certain level of communication with other people in the same line of business.

GENERATING LEADS

This is an interesting aspect of every social media website. However, it is special in Twitter because you can encourage your customers to avail themselves of your products and services by tweeting and retweeting. This way you are generating sales or are on the verge of generating sales. There are so many companies that have the offer of "Buy one get one free." They tweet this post and retweet it to ensure that they have a good amount of sales.

IMPROVING THE PERSONALITY OF YOUR BRAND

Twitter gives you the chance to improve the image of your company. You will be able to tweet about the different products and services that you provide, and will also be able to ensure that your followers know what it is that you are providing them with. You can use quirky quotes and content to grasp the attention of your followers.

RESEARCHING TRENDS

You do not have to tweet if you are using Twitter. You can also search and follow tweets to help you understand different trending topics. Twitter is the only platform that works in real time. You will be able to ensure that you are following conversations that are happening right now.

You will be able to identify the hot topic of the day and also be able to view what your customers are saying about your brand

and products. In addition, you will know what they are saying about other products in the same category.

SEEKING FEEDBACK

Many Australian companies have used Twitter and other social media to gather feedback from their customers. This is useful information for the business. You will be able to improve the business and also provide your customers with what they want. You will be able to show your potential customers that you have scope for improvement.

PROVIDE FREE CUSTOMER SERVICE

This is something that most customers adore. They would love to get service from you on the go instead of having to wait to meet you! You can have communication with your clients twenty-four hours a day. You can also have your staff answering questions that your clients have about the products that you sell. You have to work on using the right tone!

How to Market on Twitter?
Step 1: Brand Your Twitter page

When you create a Twitter page for your business, it is important that the account handle be easily recognized even without its name being visible. Follow these simple steps to set up your business Twitter profile:

1. Upload your business logo as the profile avatar. If you offer a profession service, e.g., medical consultancy, consider using a professional photo of yourself, especially if you will use Twitter to provide professional advice.

2. Upload a relevant header image. The larger banner image on your profile page should have the same theme as your website's header image.

3. Come up with a good 160-word bio text that will appear on the preview image alongside the Twitter handle, header image, profile image and external link to your website. If the business has a good slogan or motto, this is the best place to apply it.

Once you fill out all the relevant information on your Twitter profile, the page should be sleek and clean and should showcase your business or products nicely at a glance. The objective here is to attract the attention of potential followers and make it easy for them to identify the page without necessarily viewing the whole profile. While creating a professional and attractive profile is the first step in mastering marketing on Twitter, it is by no means the primary way to draw followers.

STEP 2: BUILD A NETWORK OF FOLLOWERS

Your first followers on Twitter will be people and businesses that you have interacted with via email. Twitter will prompt you to import your contacts automatically and find them on Twitter. You can easily find this tool on the "#Discover" link on top of the Twitter page and under it, "Find Friends." You can easily look up contacts from popular email services, including AOL, Yahoo, Outlook, and Gmail. Select the contacts you want to follow, or simply click on "Follow All." When you follow a contact on Twitter, they will be notified that you have followed them, and some will follow back.

You can build your Twitter fan base by first following profiles of interest. Be mindful when following Twitter users because mass following of people within a short time may cause your account to get flagged as a spammer, and it might get suspended. As a general rule, you must be observant of whom you follow on Twitter. As a business account, you should follow these rules:

1. Other businesses dealing in your industry or niche.

2. Businesses that operate in your neighborhood or city, or within your area of influence.

3. Local small business organizations and media.

4. Bloggers who regularly publish posts about your industry or products.

5. Industry publications and organizations.

Do not follow random potential customers, especially if you do so with the hope of getting follow-backs. Instead, it is a good idea to follow people and organizations that you can build relationships with. For instance, if you are a professional photographer, you can follow a local musician or wedding planning company because the relationship might benefit you.

If you have a great Twitter profile, the people you follow will eventually come to you. Establishing such a relationship is not easy, but when you contribute to sharing content through retweeting and offering useful information, links, special content, and a laugh every now and then, they will find you, retweet you, message you, and even mention you in tweets.

What to Tweet/Retweet

Just because you are microblogging, you shouldn't think that content does not matter. The content on your Twitter feed should be relevant to what you are on Twitter to achieve. Every tweet should meet at least one of these criteria:

1. Must provide useful information; e.g., an announcement, a tip, or a link to your blog posts.

2. Links to your website, blog, or other social media pages such as Facebook. About half your links should lead the reader to content you create or to your website. The other half should take them to relevant and informative publications such as news pieces, articles, commentary, reviews, or other interesting information.

3. Special offers such as price cut discounts and rewarding contests. While you should not offer your Twitter followers promo overload, you should use the platform to spread word on any special offers and promotions on offer.

4. When you announce any special events or send invitations on Facebook, be sure to tweet about them too to achieve maximum exposure.

5. Fun tweets are acceptable as well. Now and then, tweet a funny joke or meme to spread a laugh and hopefully make someone's day. However, the content of the joke

must be appropriate and entertaining. Post something that your followers might want to retweet.

6. Inspirational tweets, like laugh tweets, are not mandatory but they can go a long way in promoting sharing on social media. As always, just be sure that it is relevant and appropriate but not too generic.

WHAT NOT TO TWEET/RETWEET:

1. Unless it is relevant to your business or industry, avoid political tweets.

2. Avoid profanity and insulting tweets.

3. Never angry-tweet, period! If you have an issue with a Twitter user, try to resolve it through email or via direct messages.

4. No spam!

GENERAL TWITTER MARKETING TIPS

HASHTAGS

Hashtags (#Keyword) are the backbone of Twitter and are designed to make your posts searchable. Use a relevant hashtag with every tweet and pay attention to trending hashtags to use when appropriate. Never use more than two hashtags in a single tweet.

RETWEETS

Retweets are other people's tweets that you share with your followers. When you retweet a post, it is posted to your Twitter feed but it will show on your followers' feeds with the original tweeter's profile picture. Because the posts you retweet will appear on your profile, make sure that you only retweet relevant and appropriate content that you would tweet as your own.

COMMENTS

When you reply to tweets, they show up in a thread as comments when someone clicks the tweet. This is a great way to engage and to be discovered.

DIRECT MESSAGES

Direct messaging is a way to interact privately with a Twitter user. Use this feature when you want to engage with a user privately; for instance, to ask a specific question or respond to a customer complaint. Do not use DMs to send automated messages—not even innocuous messages such as "Thank you for following," as it can be construed as spam.

Effective social media marketing on Twitter takes a lot of work and commitment. However, when you get used to the routine of interaction and sharing, typically several times a day, it becomes a breeze. It is important that you put in valuable time in discovering where your target audience is, what is trending, and what potential customers are sharing to get in on the conversation rather than using old-fashioned marketing techniques to try get attention.

CHAPTER THIRTEEN

DOMINATE YOUTUBE MARKETING

Over the past two decades, the increased involvement of the Internet in society has shifted the strategies of small business marketing from the TV to computer screens. Any business looking to grow and promote its products can now take advantage of YouTube as a free media channel that everyone loves to love. With over 2 billion video views every day, YouTube is among the most visited sites in the world. Because it is an extremely easy and free-to-use communication channel, YouTube has emerged as the most appealing platform for video-based marketing campaigns that every entrepreneur should consider using.

BENEFITS OF USING YOUTUBE FOR BUSINESS MARKETING

You may wanted to use YouTube to enhance your marketing strategies. But before you do that, you need to understand how this media platform helps you. Once you have understood these benefits, you can use YouTube without being forced to. You will also not be too worried about the traffic to your website.

YouTube has had a rapid growth since its launch. There are people all over the world who use YouTube wherever they are able to find an Internet connection. This makes YouTube the best form of social media! It is able to ensure that an audience is generated all over the world, no matter what the purpose may be.

Over the years, people have begun to show a preference for videos over text. They tend to believe that they do not need to spend a lot of time to grasp what the content is trying to tell them. Videos are the best way to ensure that you engage and grasp the attention of a huge audience. For instance, consider a football game. Nobody these days would want to listen to the updates of the game on the radio. They would love to watch the game on a huge television.

IT HAS AN EASY INTERFACE

YouTube is by far the easiest social media platform because it very easily accessible. You have user accounts on which the content is generated based on the preference of the user. The content is also offered in various languages.

A LARGE AUDIENCE

If the video on the website is engaging, a large number of people will want to watch. If one person likes the video, there are a hundred others who may like it, too. This means there will be lot of interest in the video. You will be able to generate a large audience for the video from all over the world. This is a type of conversion! You have the possibility of generating an even bigger audience. Many people love YouTube because they are able to download and view the content on their mobile phones as well! The search engine for YouTube falls third on the list of engines. It is used by over a billion people every single day!

VIDEO OVER TEXT

As mentioned earlier, people have begun to prefer watching videos to reading texts. You are more likely to attract more people if you play an extremely good video for them. You do not have to worry about creating a bunch of content that may have no effect on the audience whatsoever. This is the reason why most websites have tried to avoid writing a lot of content and instead incorporate more videos on their pages.

A BETTER WAY TO DEMONSTRATE

When you use a video, you are able to show your viewers the exact way in which they can use a particular product or service that you are providing. This enables the customer to see the product in action, and it is more likely they will be persuaded to purchase it. If you are a one-man business, you can take a video and show the world how your service is going to benefit them.

MAKING AN IMPACT VISUALLY

The content in the video can be used to reach out to different clients and customers in a deeper manner. For instance, you may be an organization that helps children at risk. You can show them a video of how you are able to do this. That speaks louder than a bunch of content on different pages and it leaves a lasting impression on the viewers. If you have a video with the right mix of emotions, you have hit the jackpot! You can convey more through a video. It is even better if you personalize this video. It is only when you do that that people will buy into what you are trying to say to them and this will automatically generate a larger audience.

AN INEXPENSIVE MARKETING STRATEGY

When you work on making a video, you do not have to spend too much. The initial investment that you make is minimal! If you know how to make an effective video, you can just use your smartphone! There are so many devices being developed that have great camera qualities. You can use those to take videos and then use other applications that will help you enhance the quality of the videos so that you attract a larger audience.

RE-PURPOSED CONTENT

When you create a video, you can always use it in different ways. You can create podcasts or even a video series that will help you reach a larger audience. If you teach Spanish, you can have different videos where you teach the viewers different parts of Spanish. You can do the same if you know different ways to style long or short hair! You will be able to engage a lot of people with minimal effort.

EMAIL LISTING

You can work on conversions through videos too! You may want to keep a track of the leads that you have. You can do this by attaching a sign-up form that needs to be filled out by viewers when they choose to subscribe to watching your videos. This will help you increase your email listings and enable you to grow your customer base.

AdWords and AdSense

This is the program that helps a company generate money through advertisements on the website. This is always done through clicks per impression. You will be able to generate a decent income through AdWords and AdSense.

You now know the different benefits of using YouTube as a means of social media marketing. You can earn more and by spending a very small amount or no amount at all!

CREATE A YOUTUBE CHANNEL FOR YOUR BUSINESS

If your brand does not have a Google+ identity already, you will need to create one, or simply create a Gmail account to be able to sign into a YouTube channel. You will need to to to YouTube's create channel page and use your business name as the channel name.

Once your YouTube channel has been created, customize it with your brand colors, your logo as profile picture, and slogans to reinforce brand identity. It is very important at this point that you create a unified look with your website, as well as other social media channels such as Twitter and Facebook.

UNDERSTAND THE PURPOSES OF YOUTUBE VIDEOS

Before you can start uploading your videos in the hope of getting potential customers to watch, you must first get to know the three marketing purposes of YouTube videos. YouTube is often thought of as a dump of cat videos and "girls don't poop" vine clips, but the truth is that there are billions of useful videos that people watch every second of the day. Yours can be one of them.

While virality and sharing are the main purposes of sharing videos on YouTube, they are not the only reasons you should make and upload one. There are primarily three types of videos that you can create and share on your YouTube channel:

SUPPORTIVE VIDEOS

This type of video focuses on providing quality and informative content. Such a video does not really promote your brand; it supports it by conveying a simple and often emotional message.

An example is a video of your sales rep addressing a national conference or walking customers through what they need to earn a degree online.

SEO VIDEOS

Did you know that YouTube is the number two search engine after Google search and is first in the "how to" arena? Well, if your business has a shot at explaining how to achieve a goal, you can create a video on the topic and optimize it to appear top in search engine results.

SHARING IS CARING VIDEOS

These are often clever, fun, emotional, or useful videos that are meant to be shared.

CREATE QUALITY YOUTUBE VIDEOS

When you have settled on the type and content of video to create for marketing purposes, take some time to do research on the keywords to use. You can browse similar videos on YouTube to get ideas on best practices, keywords, titles and terms to use. To help you along, you need to think like your target user and make the kind of video that you would like to see, and at the same time think like a marketer to make sure you do not stray away from the core purpose of the video.

When you have the raw video footage, you can use free tools such as iMovie, Windows Movie Maker, Wideo, or YouTube's inbuilt video editor to edit the video and get it ready for publication. You will also need to take a crash course on how to apply annotations, YouTube cards, embedded links, and call-to-action overlays to make your video more effective in persuading viewers to carry out a desired action, such as sign up for your newsletter, subscribe to your channel, or share the video.

OPTIMIZE YOUR VIDEO FOR SEARCH ENGINES

1. Your video should have a metro targeted keyword phrase in the title. For instance, if you are a freelance photographer in Los Angeles, the phrase "Photographer in Los Angeles" should appear once on the title of the video.

However, be sure that the phrase you use is relevant to the content of the video.

2. Optimize the video by ensuring that the targeted keyword phrase appears in the description. YouTube allows you enter a description of up to 500 to 600 words in the description area; craft it so that the keywords appear at the beginning of the description. Use a range of long tail keyword phrase variations creatively throughout the description.

3. Use up to ten relevant tags that identify the video to users and search engines. The tags should include the video category, names of people featured, products, content type, location, etc. Tags help YouTube viewers decide whether a video is worth their time.

4. Upload a transcript for every video that you upload. A transcript is text of the words spoken in the video. If your video talks about your brand, products, or services in the

local market, an audio transcript will reinforce the relevance and the authority of the video.

5. Set a catchy but relevant custom thumbnail image for your video. A custom thumbnail gives people an idea what the video is about even before they visit your channel or the video page. This is very important because it helps your video stand out in search results, catching the attention of Google users and helping boost the video's click through rates.

6. Finally, since you want every video you upload to be viewed and shared across all social media channels, include social sharing and embedding links on the video to facilitate easier and faster sharing. The easiest way to make embedding your video simple is to create a landing page on your website or blog, then post the video on that page.

If all of this is too complicated for you, then it is best to avail the help of someone who knows how to do everything. It is best to trust a professional instead of going about it with half knowledge.

PROMOTE YOUR VIDEO

Promoting YouTube videos primarily involves encouraging viewers to watch your videos, like and comment on them, and subscribe to your channel so that they can see your videos on their feed whenever you upload one. How do you promote your videos and YouTube channel?

One way to promote your YouTube videos is through *cross-promotion*. This is linking your social media accounts to your website. Your videos should have a link to your website in the description and, when you publish a blog post, a link to your video should be included. You should also share your videos on Twitter and Facebook and any other social media site. Search engines consider shared videos popular and this encourages other users to view and share them.

You can also pay to have YouTube suggest your videos to people matching certain criteria you set. At the beginning, when your channel is new and you have very few video views and even fewer subscribers and are trying to get your view count up, you can opt for paid advertising. Early advertising will get you lots of organic traffic later on and Google will pay attention to your videos and channel from there onwards.

CHAPTER FOURTEEN

DOMINATE INSTAGRAM MARKETING

Successfully setting up an Instagram account for your business is just the first step toward utilizing this powerful visual social media platform as a marketing tool. To stand out and dominate on Instagram, you need to have a lot of influence, many followers, and many customers. Engagement on Instagram is as high as 15 times more than the interaction on Facebook; it is a platform no serious small business entrepreneur can afford to ignore. Your Instagram marketing strategy should focus on making your brand more engaging and consistent to build trust and showcase your products and expertise. This chapter walks you through the straightforward process of leveraging Instagram to market your business and products, and it begins with you knowing your target market.

STEP 1: PICK THE RIGHT INSTAGRAM USERNAME

When picking a username for your business Instagram account, try to use the business name that customers can easily identify. Instagram is a fast-growing social network, so if you find that your business name is already taken, you can still use one of the several suggestions that Instagram comes up with, which will include your original preferred username with numbers added. However, industry experts agree that using your location abbreviation or punctuation comes across as more presentable and professional.

STEP 2: SET UP YOUR PROFILE

Once you have your business's Instagram username set, the next step is to complete the bio section of the profile. For people to find your business's profile on Instagram, you must make the bio section count. You have just 150 characters to work with;

therefore, you must be as creative as possible. Make sure that the description includes the strongest industry and location keywords in order to make your account easy to find through the app's search tool and search engines.

Because your profile is the only place where you can place a clickable link, always include a call to action and a link to your website. Most users prefer to use a third party app (e.g., Notes on iPhone) to add special formatting and spacing of text on their Instagram profile to give it a unique look. You should too.

STEP 3: LEARN TO POST WHAT PEOPLE WANT

Once you have set up your profile, you are ready to start sharing. Your Instagram marketing campaign will only be successful when you have a clear purpose for every post. It is best to get to know your target audience first and find out what kind of images they want to see. This you can do by seeing what they like in general. Keep it along the same lines. Trying to vary things too much might mean experimenting. And, if you are still in the initial stages of setting up your profile, it is better to play safe than to experiment too much. Always use high-quality, original, and sharp images to convey a professional image. It is also imperative that you are consistent with the type of images you post—try to keep your personal and business profiles separate.

Determine what visual style you should brand your business with and stick to it. Is there a particular image angle or filter you always use? Perhaps you have a particular photo style you can stick to? Make it easy for your audience to identify and brand your images by being consistent with the type, style, and nature of the images you share. This will go a long way toward helping your business branding efforts.

STEP 4: HAVE A SOLID HASHTAG STRATEGY

The only way to make your content searchable and discoverable on Instagram is by using hashtags. You should therefore make learning to use hashtags a priority. I recommend that you come up with a hashtag strategy for your account, which involves first getting familiar with the hashtags suitable for your industry and identifying unique hashtags to use for your business. Using relevant hashtags will make it easy for people to curate, search and find the content you are sharing.

Once you have a hashtag to use in your Instagram marketing campaign, encourage your fans to use it whenever they post images related to your business or products. This will go a long way to help their followers track back the hashtag to your account. You should include a minimum of five to seven hashtags in the description section of each post to reach new users. The important consideration when using hashtags is to choose those that help your followers not only organize and categorize images and videos, but also discover new content. No one can tolerate hashtag stuffing. A brand that fills a post with unrelated hashtags is just annoying.

STEP 5: OPTIMIZE YOUR POSTS

All your Instagram posts should include clear calls to action (CTAs) that may appear on the image itself or on the caption. Just as with hashtags and image types, you should be consistent in how you include the call to action. Some Instagram users prefer to embed the CTA text on the image itself, while others have it on the description.

Another important strategy to optimize your Instagram posts for your marketing campaign is to use the geotagging tool to add location for calls to action, especially if you run a location-based business. The best part about using geotagging for your posts is that Instagram will create a photo map of your posts and make viewing your previous posts an adventure for new and existing followers.

Vary Post Caption Length. Instagram is primarily a photo sharing social network, but it is possible to use it to share text content. For each Instagram post, you can include up to 2,000 characters of caption, which to many users is sufficient space for a paragraph or two of quality content. There is a lot of power in the written word, and if you need to tell a story to promote your brand, go ahead and use this section to make your voice heard. Try alternating short and long captions to discover which type of text content best resonates with your target audience and settle on a winner.

STEP 6: ENGAGE WITH YOUR FOLLOWERS, ONLINE AND OFFLINE

Sharing great images and videos on Instagram is just one step in the long journey toward winning followers and building a community; to win customers, you must go a step further and engage with the community you have formed. The best approach is to get the most out of your Instagram campaign by engaging with customers and encouraging employees to do the same. The many ways of interacting with your Instagram followers online include:

TAGS

Instagram allows you to add tags to an image or video before you publish it, just like Facebook does. Tag users using the "Tag People" option, then select the people you wish to tag before publishing the photo. The people you tag on the photo will be notified and other users can see who is tagged on it.

MENTIONS

Mentions on Instagram work a lot like mentions on Twitter. To mention users, simply use the @ symbol before the user's Instagram username in the comment or caption section of the image or video. Mentions are also used when replying to a person's comment in the comments section of the image or video.

LIKES

The simplest way to connect with other users on Instagram is through likes. You can like a photo by double tapping it or by tapping the heart button just below the post.

COMMENTS

Comments on posts appear at the bottom of the image or video. To comment, simply tap the *Comment* button and the app will take you to the comments page. A textbox where you can type your comment will appear; when you are ready to publish, simply press *Send*.

DIRECT MESSAGING

The Instagram Direct feature is a tool that users can use to communicate privately. This tool allows you to send text messages, photos, and videos to other users without making them available publicly. If you send a direct message to a user who is not already following you, they will first be asked whether they want to allow you to send them messages, videos, and images before they can view the direct message.

STEP 7: CONNECT YOUR INSTAGRAM TO YOUR OTHER SOCIAL CHANNELS

Get more bang for your buck and increase your followers by linking your Instagram account with your other social networks; i.e., Facebook, Twitter, etc. This way, whenever you share any image or video on Instagram, it will be automatically posted to these profiles, allowing your fans on Facebook and followers on Twitter to see your Instagram stream and like, comment, or share your content. This is a sure way to reach the widest audience and boost brand recognition through interconnected social media marketing.

CHAPTER FIFTEEN

DOMINATE LINKEDIN MARKETING

LinkedIn is the go-to social networking site for professionals in every industry. This is a dynamic and revolutionary professional networking site that small business entrepreneurs can use to boost their businesses, and even increase sales.

If you are not familiar with LinkedIn, or still think it as just a website for people hunting for jobs, you have a pretty steep learning curve to cover in order to harness the full potential of the site as a marketing tool for small businesses.

LinkedIn, unlike other social sites we have discussed already, doesn't have "personal pages." An individual's page is all about the industry they are trained in, the experience they have, and the work they do.

How to use LinkedIn For Small Business Marketing

LinkedIn is the ultimate marketing hub for social marketing executives as well as solopreneurs. According to LinkedIn Business, a significant number of American small business entrepreneurs, with 200 or fewer employees, have used LinkedIn to find new customers, grow their revenue, and promote their brand over the last year. A recent Wall Street Journal study showed that 41% of small businesses found LinkedIn to be a potent tool for generating leads and new business contacts.

LinkedIn Social Media Marketing Goals for Small Businesses

A LinkedIn profile today is a business's or a professional's business card. When you decide to use LinkedIn to promote your business, your core business goals would be to:

1. Create new and expand existing relationships with key contacts and with your network.

2. Build professional credibility with quality content.

3. Expand the reach of your brand by leveraging your employee base.

LinkedIn is a popular social media platform for professionals and, just like other social media platforms, it has a social contract with its members as well as key use cases. This is not a sales channel or a place where you can just promote your coupons. The site has become more of a publishing and editorial channel that entrepreneurs can make use of to build an evangelizing workforce, connect with professionals who need their products and services, and connect with local business owners who will most likely support other business owners they know.

STEP 1: CREATE A LINKEDIN COMPANY PAGE

To get started on LinkedIn, create your professional profile if you do not have one already. A profile on LinkedIn is pretty basic. You will need to fill in your basic data, including your professional background, experience, skills, education, certifications, organizations you are involved with, projects, awards, publications, patents, and courses. Enhance your profile by uploading a professional photo and using images, videos, and document attachments to enhance the various sections.

When your personal profile is complete, you can then create a profile for your business. A business profile will amplify your brand's image to customers, association members, distributors and other professionals and business owners. On your business page, highlight the services and products you offer and connections with your employees and your leadership to build external credibility and a community. The important thing is to include as much information as possible about the business in the profile to make it easy for users to find it and to make it appear complete and professional.

STEP 2: RUN PERSONAL AND BUSINESS LINKEDIN PAGES AS A CAMPAIGN

The best social media marketing strategy to adopt on LinkedIn is to run your professional and business profiles as SEO and PPC campaigns. The objective here is to make your pages easy to find on search engines such as Google. The search engine optimization component ensures that customers find your LinkedIn pages when they search certain keywords. By running your pages as campaigns, you increase the company's credibility and "findability." The keywords you use in the profile headline, in the summary sections, the job descriptions, anchored texts, and endorsements play a big role in getting your page optimized for search engines.

STEP 3: DISCOVER AND JOIN LINKEDIN GROUPS WITH LOCAL TIES

Statistics from LinkedIn show that an average user joins between seven and ten LinkedIn groups. This means that it is easier for you to find your influencers, competitors, and customers in the LinkedIn communities they are members of. Over 75 percent of customers use LinkedIn groups to get maximum exposure to other group members sharing the same interest.

To take advantage of this in your marketing campaign, you will need to do some research on the groups, networks, and communities that members of your target audience join to be accessible by the members. Your business profile should be a member of between 70 and 100 groups. However, joining groups and forming communities is not enough. Stay active by regularly participating in non-promotional activities and by forming individual relationships with other business owners, distributors, and the local press.

STEP 4: BLOG ON LINKEDIN

By now, you know that blogging is by far the most potent way to create marketing content, as the largest percentage of customers are influenced by blog posts. It therefore makes sense that your LinkedIn marketing campaign includes publishing blog posts on your blog, on LinkedIn, and on other social networking sites. Because you are connecting with different audiences on your blog and on LinkedIn, you can use the same content on each site. This will help build the brand's credibility and establish the page as an active and reliable profile to network with.

STEP 5: CREATE NEW CONNECTIONS

Once you have your business's LinkedIn profile set, it will prompt you to locate your existing contacts by importing your email contacts. With this tool, you can easily find your fellow high school and college alumni, past employees and workmates, and professional contacts. Based on your networks, the system will also recommend people you might know such as people from your location, users with similar industry backgrounds, and even connections of your connections.

Note, however, that LinkedIn discourages connecting with people you don't know. Choose your connections with care and avoid sending random connect invites to avoid being limited to using email addresses to send connect requests in the future.

STEP 6: SECURE LINKEDIN ENDORSEMENTS AND RECOMMENDATIONS

Positive endorsements on LinkedIn have a great influence on many users' purchase decisions. Employees, suppliers, customers, and everyone else can use these personal endorsements to build the reputation of your small business. Getting recommendations for both your personal and business LinkedIn profiles is also a great way to be part of "word-of-mouth" marketing strategy because these recommendations are as effective as referrals; the more you get, the greater the business's reputation.

STEP 7: SEND REGULAR STATUS UPDATES

The simplest way to create updates for your business LinkedIn page is to post all your blog posts as updates. LinkedIn will post the blog post as an update with a nice thumbnail image from the blog post. You can also update the LinkedIn status with important business information, such as event and business news, links to articles mentioning your business, and even an occasional inspirational quote. It is imperative that your page remains active but, unlike other social networks, LinkedIn is not a place to post an occasional joke, meme, or funny clips to keep your connections entertained. All your updates should strictly focus on business and providing valuable and relevant information.

CHAPTER SIXTEEN

GENERAL TIPS ON USING SOCIAL MEDIA

PERSONAL LEVEL

The first and foremost point to note before you start using social media is that you have to portray your company as a person and not an innate thing. You have to speak to your customers via your company's profile in such a way that they think a real person is interacting with them. So, when you create a profile, think like a person and not a company owner. Make yourself the company and interact with your customers to help convert leads into customers.

LISTENING IS KEY

It is extremely important that you listen to everything that your customers have to say about you and your company. You cannot listen only to positive feedback and ignore the negative feedback. It is understood that positivity will help you flourish, but not paying heed to the negative feedback will push you down and make you feel like you are not worthy of people's praises, so it is important that you listen to any advice that you get from anyone and use it to your advantage.

UNIFORMITY

It is vital to maintain consistent uniformity amongst all your social media platforms. They should be interconnected and people should recognize you from one place to the other. And don't think being strong in any one of the platforms is enough for your business to grow. You have to remain present in all platforms, since the same people might not be present everywhere. You will thereby increase your potential reach and interact with as many different people as possible. Try to maintain a uniform theme all throughout and campaign in a similar fashion.

INFORMATION

It is extremely important for you to provide your customers with important information that will be of use to them. If you are trying to tell them something that they already know and not giving any new information, it will be pretty useless. It is like reading a book that is telling you everything that you already know. Your social media presence should be built on trust and people must relate with you for providing them with day-to-day information that will help them lead a better, and simpler, life.

COMPETITIONS

All social media platforms are great places for you to host competitions. These competitions need not be on a large scale; even a small-scale competition will generate people's interest. You have to announce interesting competitions and, more important, interesting prizes. These prizes should be valuable to the end user and should go beyond logo printed merchandize. Once you get people to participate, you will see that more and more are willing to participate in it and will bring their friends along as well. This means a larger audience and more people looking at your brand. You have to time these competitions well and make sure that word of them reaches your customers, every single time.

IF THIS, THEN THAT

No, I am not talking about IFTTT here; I'm only talking about tie-ups. Tie-ups refer to you tying up with other companies and their products. Many times, you will come across schemes where buying a product of one company will give you a discount on the product of another company. Similarly, you can tie up with a company that sells a product similar to yours, and then announce to your customers that they can get a 5% or 10% off on the other product if they buy yours.

EVENTS

You have to organize events from time to time and announce them on your media platforms. These events should create awareness of your social media platforms and the advantages of signing up with you. Choose a location that is close to your main audiences and give them instructions on how they can reach there. You must organize food and drinks and also giveaways to those that attend the event. You can then address them and allow them to interact with each other. Such rapport building will go a very long way in helping you establish a strong connect with your online customers.

FEEDBACK

Don't forget to ask them for their feedback. They have to tell you what they liked and did not like about the event. Collect all the feedback from them and go through it closely. It will contain instructions on where you need to make improvements. You can then implement these changes and further satisfy your customers.

They will be happy to see that their advice has been taken seriously and their opinions have mattered.

DEDICATED TEAM

You have to have a dedicated team that takes care of all your online promotions. This team must be well versed in the ways of the Internet and know exactly what to do to promote your company. When you assemble the team, it must include an engineer, a social media expert, and someone who has an eye for detail. You can find the right people online and hiring freelancers is a good option. Check out places like fiverr, where you will find people willing to work for you for $5 or less. Once your team comes up with the content, you must approve it before it goes live. You must ask them to reply to every query that people post and customize the replies.

PROMOTIONS

You have to indulge in unique promotional strategies to promote your brand and strategies. If you use run-of-the-mill strategies, nobody will fancy it. Your promotions should be one of a kind and unique. You must raise people's curiosity and get them to explore whatever you offer them. One interesting promotion idea is to bring back some piece of nostalgia. It can be an old advertisement that was popular back in the day or revive a product that was once a best-seller. All of these will help you remain popular.

COLLABORATE

It is a good idea to collaborate with other bloggers and people who are popular on the web. That will give you the chance to attract their customers and your popularity will increase. Apart from asking them to mention you in their posts, you can also get them to write something for you. You can also collaborate and create unique products that capture your ideas and theirs effectively.

QUALITY AND QUANTITY

When using social media, you have to focus on both quality and quantity of your posts. Focusing on just one will not cut it for you. Quality refers to the content that you provide. Whether it is a blog or an eBook, you must concentrate on content that is worthy of the reader. If they are not satisfied with it, they will not consider returning, so it is important that you get it right and satisfy your readers. Secondly, quantity is important. You have to keep updating information from time to time. If you forget about it, then so will your customers and that is not an ideal situation. You have to choose topics that are trending and write interesting articles on it.

OPPORTUNISTIC

You have to remain opportunistic. You must look for opportunities to exploit in the social media arena. If there is scope to attract a certain type of audience, then you must jump at it. It takes a keen eye to spot an opportunity and you must remain ready at all times. Your social media team will come in handy at such times and help you scour for opportunities to capitalize upon.

FLEXIBLE

Remain as flexible as possible when it comes to modifying your schemes and campaigns. Nobody knows what might come next and it is important to be ready for anything. Flexibility is vital when it comes to establishing strength.

CLEAN UP

If you have a bad image on the Internet now, owing to some mistakes that you made, don't worry, you can fix it by indulging in clean-ups. You can clean up your image by consulting an expert and asking for tips on how to do it. Start by looking at all the negative comments that people have posted and why they are there. Act on them and, if it is possible, delete them. If it is not, improve your service and get people to comment positively, which will help you clean up at least some of your image.

Keeping the Audience Happy

It is extremely important that you keep your audience happy when you are trying to capitalize on social media platforms. In this segment, we will look at what you can do to keep your target audience satisfied.

INVITE THEM

The very first thing to do is to invite people. How will someone know about you if you don't send those invites to your pages? Whether it is Facebook or Twitter, you must tell people that you are there. One way of doing it is by having the information printed on boxes or covers that you give them when they buy your products. You can slip in a thank-you card with details of your social media presence printed on it. It is also a good idea to send personnel to propagate the message in malls and other such public places, so that people know of your existence.

SATISFY THEM

Once they check you out, you must satisfy them. Give them what they want. They have to feel happy about accessing you and being satisfied with the experience. Apart from important and useful information, you must also provide them with something that they will cherish. Maybe a 15% coupon from your store is a good way to start. If they like you, then they are sure to return. Similarly, have something waiting for them when they arrive at your designated social media page. When you know that someone has actually redeemed their coupon, you can surmise that they are in your target audience.

STALK THEM

Once you identify this target, you must literally stalk them. You must keep an eye on them and see what they are up to. This information you can get from their social media profiles and interactions. Most companies limit it to wishing these customers a happy birthday once a year and don't go beyond that. But you must do more. If they have recently achieved something, then you must duly congratulate them and send them a tailored message. Customizing such messages will make your customers happy and they will be happy to associate with you. But don't overdo any of it, as that can get a little annoying.

EMAIL

You must send emails from time to time. But apart from mentioning any new products that are available with you, you must also ask them about their response to any products that they have bought from you. You must be available 24 hours to solve any problems, and also have a team ready to demonstrate or set up the product. All of this will go a very long way in your customers developing a strong bond with you.

PROBLEM SOLVING

One important aspect to understand is how problem solving will work in your favor. When you wish to solve a problem that your customer is having, you must immediately cite an example of your rival company, and tell them how they do not provide customers with such quick problem solving. This will help to increase their trust in you. After all, in this day and age where competition is sky high, you must do everything in your power to win your customers' trust.

SPECIAL OFFERS

One important strategy to make use of on social media is "special offers." These special offers must be available only on your social media platforms and not anywhere else, including your stores. This will lure them to buy from the links that you have sprinkled all over your social media platforms.

These are various points that you must bear in mind when you wish to use social media as your platform for all your marketing needs.

THE 80/20 ANALYSIS

The 80/20 analysis is one of the most important statistical tools that you must use to assess your performance on social media platforms. As you know, it is important to keep tab of your progress and know what is working for you and what is not.

One good way of doing it is through 80/20 analysis. The 80/20 analysis is one of the most used statistical tools in the world. It will help you know what is working for you and what is not.

The 80/20 analysis stands for a very simple principle. The principle states that 80% of your business comes from 20% of input. This 20% is a variable and can stand for products, customers, employees, etc.

So if you have two products, A and B, and one of them is doing well and the other not so much, then you will easily know which product is giving you 80% sales.

That is just a small sample space where only two products are present. Now imagine what would happen in a large space, where 100 products are available.

In such a case, the 80/20 analysis will come in handy. As per the analysis, you make use of a statistical calculation to arrive at the 20% that is contributing to your business in a big way.

You can apply this principle to your social media networks and find out which one is doing well for you.

The calculation is pretty simple. Start by writing down the number of customers that you have, who are your social media finds.

Next, write down the total number of people from each medium next to the name of the medium. For example, if you have 100,000 likes on Facebook, then write that down next to Facebook.

Similarly, write down all the values next to the names, preferably in descending order. Next to these values, you must write down the total number of customers that you have. Once you do, you can divide the latter into the former and arrive at a number. Depending on the ratio, you will see which one has the highest number and which one has the lowest.

The one with the highest is your most successful platform and the lowest is your least successful.

Say, for example, you get 30% for Twitter and 12% for LinkedIn. You must pay close attention to your LinkedIn account to see how you can improve it.

This 80/20 analysis should be conducted from time to time and you must capitalize on the platform that is working for you and boost the one that is not faring too well.

CHAPTER SEVENTEEN

ADVERTISING

AFFILIATE MARKETING

Imagine there is a fair in town. You know you make the best cupcakes this town has ever seen. You've also received praise from your townspeople and now you think it's time for you to expand your small business and this fair presents you with an opportunity to bring in new customers. So you set up a stall and bring out your best cupcakes. There are three ways through which you can attract new customers. You can scream and shout and say you have the best cupcakes to offer. Another way is to wait for your loyal customers to bring in new customers by word-of-mouth advertising. But the most efficient and easiest way is to join with another stall owner and make a deal that is mutually satisfactory. You could agree to give the other owner a small discount off of every customer that comes to your stall through his reference by selling goods at discounted rates but make profit in sales volume. This type of marketing is seen in social media marketing too. It is called affiliate marketing. Though it is a very old form of marketing, it is still being used by many websites.

Replace the fair in the above mentioned analogy with social media networking sites, the cupcakes and your stall with your product and website, the other stall owner with another website owner, and you have the basic principle behind affiliate marketing: forging relationships. The three main parties that make up the relationship in affiliate marketing are:

1. The Advertiser

2. The Publisher, aka the affiliate

3. The Customer

First, let us put you in the role of the advertiser and look at affiliate marketing from that perspective. Before anything, you need to scout out other websites that have relevant products that are connected to your product. For example, let us assume that you have started a dog grooming business. You should collect information on all websites that are related to dogs: animal shelters, rescue homes, vet clinics etc. Narrow it down till you get to one website or very few websites you trust. For this, you can look at how many people visit the website/s you've chosen and how popular it is and whether the websites deliver. Or another way to find this information to do a simple Google search. For example, you could place the following phrase into the Google search engine: "product name + affiliate program." Replace product name with the name of the product you are promoting, and this should bring you to the landing page, as many major websites have an affiliate program. Then you contact the owner of the website and come up with a deal that will entail you giving them the advertisement containing a link and them posting it. The deal will also include an understanding of payment. To make this type of advertising more enticing, the deal will also include a type of discount. The publisher will provide your link on their website and the offer is that if the viewer lands on your page through the publisher's link, the viewer will get a free voucher or a discount of some sort. To keep track of such traffic, you should give the publisher a unique tracking affiliate link so you will know how much traffic that website has brought you.

TYPES OF PAYMENTS

Now you need to pay the affiliate for his services. There are many types of compensation that are available. A few of them are mentioned below.

REVENUE SHARING

Here, the cost of advertising is determined by the revenue generated as a result of the advertisement itself. You pay the affiliate just for the fact that your link has been advertised on his website. This is very risky method because you might be paying a publisher who hasn't brought in any form of business for you. Would you pay somebody for not doing the work they were supposed to? No. But as you start out as a small business, you cannot make demands so it is safer to not sign deals with publishers who ask for this method of compensation. This method is rarely used.

COST PER CLICK (CPC)

Every time you get notified that a visitor has used the publisher's link to land on your page, you pay the publisher. It is just as the name says – for every click on your link, you pay the affiliate. This again might prove to be a bit problematic, as people could have accidentally clicked your link. You haven't gotten any proper business but, since the link was used, you have to pay the affiliate.

COST PER MILLE (CPM)

This is closely related to revenue sharing but much cheaper for you as an advertiser. Here you pay the affiliate for every 1000 views his website, which includes your advertisement, gets.

COST PER ACTION (CPA)

This method of payment is by far the most relevant and useful. Here, there is another process that comes into play to see if the affiliate gets paid or not. The visitor cannot just click on the link and land on your page but a conversion needs to happen. This can be brought about by the visitor filling some questionnaire or giving some details about himself so you have a solid lead to follow. Only when this conversion happens can the affiliate be paid.

There are certain things that you should keep in mind when you start off in affiliate marketing. You cannot expect results overnight. The basis of affiliate marketing is relationships and it takes time to build them. You can still advertise on many websites in order to make your presence felt, but it is advisable to stop with one or very few websites. It is, after all, quality over quantity. It is better to get into business with one website that has a higher rate of conversions rather than many that will have less or no results. Another thing to remember is that affiliate marketing is merely marketing. The affiliate can only bring the consumer to your website. You should have products that are good and a website that grabs the attention of your visitor that s/he is tempted to do business with you. Affiliate marketing cannot take care of sales on its own. It is merely a step towards sales. You should also keep an eye on your affiliate. Uncontrolled affiliates can drive your potential consumers away by spamming through cookies or indulge in false advertisements.

ADSENSE

Would you like to earn money by doing nothing? Who wouldn't, right? Then sign up with AdSense, a contextual ad network, owned by Google. This means that ads that are related to your blog will appear. And the best part? You get paid for those ads.

To make use of AdSense, you should first see if your blog is compatible with AdSense. To figure this out, read AdSense's Terms of Service, as there are certain niches that AdSense will not cater to.

HOW TO CREATE AN ADSENSE ACCOUNT

First you sign up with your existing Gmail address, or you can create an account and then sign up. Step 2 consists of filling out a very straightforward form. Care should be taken that you do not add the http:// while entering your blog address. In step 3, "payee name" is very important and you should enter your name as it appears in your bankbook because AdSense will pay you by sending a check with that name or an electronic fund transfer under that name. This is important, as there are certain countries that do not let you change payee name after signing up. The following are the countries that do not allow any changes after signing up:

Algeria

Bangladesh

Bahrain

Brazil

Egypt

Sri Lanka

China

India

Jordan

Indonesia

Kuwait

Libya

Malaysia

Lebanon

Saudi Arabia

Morocco

Oman

Nepal

Pakistan

Philippines

Palestine

Qatar

Singapore

Thailand

Tunisia

United Arab Emirates

Vietnam

Yemen

Fill in all the other details under contact information and read the AdSense policies. Do not just put a checkmark against all the boxes but take time to read the policies, because Google adheres strictly to its rules and even a small mistake can lead to termination of your account. For fast approval, use a domain-specific email address. After you submit the form, you will need to add the AdSense codes to your blog and then the AdSense team will review your application and activate your account. Once you earn your first $10, AdSense will send you a PIN. After everything is done, you should send in your tax information and enter your PIN.

There are certain things you must keep from doing to keep your account safe. You cannot ask your friends and family to click on the ads on your page, nor can you send the ads via email. Make sure all the links you provide on your blog are sites whose content is not objectionable to AdSense: for example, pornography, racial content, violent content, etc. Do not place your ads on the content of your blog so that readers are forced to click on the link. AdSense will not tolerate any of this and will definitely deactivate your account.

AdSense will not show more than three content ads on a page and it follows the method of PPC (pay per click); it will pay you once you reach $100 in earnings. It pays 68% of revenue to the publisher (you) and the remaining 32% it takes for itself to maintain and develop new technology. AdSense also makes use of CTR to finalize your payment. CTR stands for "click through rate." It is basically the ratio of the number of clicks on advertisement to the number of page views.

AdSense can also be used for search wherein it boosts your earning and also helps readers to find content within your blog.

There are two options for AdSense for search: you can show results on a Google page or on your blog page. It is advisable to keep the search within your blog as it lowers the bounce rate.

AdSense vs. Affiliate Marketing:

There is no doubt that affiliate marketing is more beneficial than AdSense. Though AdSense gives you recurring income, one affiliate sometimes pays more. Affiliate ads give you control over your ads. You can design the ads and make them look however you want, but in AdSense you have no control over what might appear on your blog. Affiliate marketing doesn't need a complex set of procedures and it is easier to get into, which cannot be said for AdSense. There are also many affiliate marketers, while AdSense is managed by Google alone. But you should know one thing—if you have a business website that is just starting up; you might want to hold back on getting in with AdSense.

AdSense is a contextual ad network, as was mentioned before. This means that you will be showing your potential clients other websites that give the same good that you do. You are providing your competition with opportunities to grab customers. You are actually losing visitors because when they click on the ad they are taken to another page. They can easily come back to your page but it is not guaranteed.

ADWORDS

AdWords is another online advertising service that is owned by Google. Here, you can advertise through Google on a budget. This type of advertising is based on keywords and your ad will appear on SERP (search engine results page). You can choose where your ads appear and set a budget you're comfortable with and, when people enter your keyword, your website link will appear above the Google search results or on the right-hand side of the page under "Sponsored Links."

As the basic idea is the keyword, each keyword you choose will have a cost per click bid amount where you specify the maximum amount you are willing to pay every time your ad gets clicked. The more you bid, the higher your ad will be placed on the page.

Let us assume, again, that you own a dog grooming service. You also provide everything related to dogs, like their food, dog training, dog mating, etc. If somebody searches for a dog trainer, your website will also be placed as an ad as somewhere your keywords match.

The various advantages of using AdWords is that you will reach potential leads because your ad appears only when people search for the likes if your product. Also, you will be charged only when someone clicks on your ad, as AdWords follow CPC.

For your ad to appear on SERP, you will need to bid against rival websites on how much you will pay Google AdWords every time a visitor clicks on your ad But most of the times it is not just the bids that Google looks at. It uses a technique called "quality score" where Google looks at how relevant your ad is to the keywords you've provided.

There is another lesser-used option called CPM (cost per mille) where you pay Google for every 1,000 times your ad appears on the results page. This doesn't take into account whether the searcher clicks on the ad or not.

A major disadvantage with AdWords is that you pay for clicks. It doesn't matter if the searcher who has landed on your page buys anything or not. AdWords will get your money just because someone clicked it. Small start-ups are at a disadvantage because major companies have a lot of cash flow and would have already locked down on general terms. For example, if your start-up concerns itself with herbal products, other already existing big companies would have taken terms like "natural," etc., and you would have to spend at least $5 for a click on that term; and, since the competitor has more money, he will bid higher and get placed on the top of the SERP. Another drawback is that AdWords have a word limit. It allows only 25 characters in the headline, 35 characters each in the two lines of text below the headline, and another 35 characters for the URL.

AdWords vs. AdSense

The main difference between the two is that while AdSense pays you, you have to pay AdWords. AdWords is used by advertisers and allows you to advertise on major search engines, whereas AdSense is used by publishers who advertise other websites on their own websites. AdWords users have flexibility because they can control what content will appear on their ad but AdSense users have no control over the content of the ad.

KEY HIGHLIGHTS

This book is a guide for all beginners in social media marketing and a refresher for those who have prior experience! You will be able to relate to the concepts that you read and you can identify where you have gone wrong and what you can do to correct your mistakes.

The book is divided into two parts. The first part dealt with the different aspects that need to be considered when marketing on social media. It provided you with the essential steps that you need to follow in order to ensure that you stay on top when it comes to social media marketing. You saw how the book flowed like water and everything fell into place.

The first chapter of the first part dealt with helping you understand what the power of social media is. You learnt about the three main components of social media, and how social media marketing is beneficial when compared to any other form of marketing. I'm sure you are convinced that social media is the best place for you to start with marketing your brand.

The next chapter is where you began to understand what goes into social media marketing. You learnt about the importance of keywords when you are using social media as your platform for marketing. You were told about the different reasons why keywords are important, and how you can use them to increase your reach. You have also been provided with a short procedure that you should follow to ensure that you have the best set of keywords. You then learnt about the importance of search engine optimization, or SEO. It is essential that you optimize your website so it will catch the eye of the various search engines that are used. If you think you are not adept at it, then you must seek help to get started and continue on from there.

We then looked at blogging in detail and saw how you must use your blog to reach out to people. It should be a combination of quality and quantity, and you must keep updating your blog from time to time. Write about interesting topics so that you build traffic. Then sprinkle your blog with links to your website. Each link should take the person to a different page on your website, and you must then entice the person to buy something from you.

You then learnt about how good your content must be on social media to ensure that visitors read it. You were given tips on how to ensure that this is done with ease! It is essential that you memorize the techniques provided, since they will help you gain more views. You were then told how you will need to work on promoting the content that you post on the website, or on any social media.

Next, conversions and lead nurturing were explained. It is essential that you keep track of all the people visiting your page and making the effort to sign up to avail themselves of your offer. You must ensure that you work on maintaining a good rapport with your consumers. It is only through them that you will be able to gather a larger group of consumers. The best way to remain connected with them is by understanding them thoroughly. You have to make the effort to know them personally and understand their wants and needs. Once you do that, you can send them emails about products and services that are to their taste. They will feel elated, as you will do half their job for them. They will then turn into your regular customers and through word of mouth you will end up getting more.

The world works so much on smartphones these days! You were told about how you will need to ensure that you are on mobile networks, too! You need to have content that will look good on mobile phones, and you also learnt about how you can ensure that you maintain a hold on the people who view your website on their mobile phones. The last chapter in the first part dealt with the ways in which you will need to analyze your strategies to ensure that you gather a good amount of traffic. All of these tips are important to pursue and will ensure that you have a successful run at it.

The second part of the book provided you with details of how you need to ensure that you have the best marketing strategies on the various social media platforms – Facebook, Twitter, YouTube, Instagram, and LinkedIn.

Firstly, we looked at Facebook marketing in detail and saw why it is one of the most preferred social media platforms used by companies to promote their brands and products. We saw how Facebook is home to billions of people and how even a small ad there can get you noticed by all the right people. Obtaining leads is extremely easy on Facebook and you will have the chance to convert your regular users into customers. A Facebook page is a very powerful tool. You can easily reach your target audience by making use of it. But care must be taken while creating one, because your page must be true to your company. You must employ someone to update the page from time to time and get as many people to like it as possible. The main aim is to get noticed and, who knows, you might get liked by an influential person who will end up bringing in a lot of business to you. And once you do, you have to keep track of how many people are now liking and following you and whether all of them are your regular customers.

Next, we looked at how Twitter can be used as a powerful tool to market your brand and products. Twitter, as you know, is a microblogging site with millions of registered users all over the world. So, just by tweeting a simple message, you can communicate with someone located on the other side of the globe. But the main advantage of using Twitter is in getting research about the top trends in the country. Every day, many different topics will start trending on the Internet and all of them will be discussed on Twitter. People will give each one a name and then place a hashtag before it. You can make use of this and start tweeting using the same hashtag. You can end up being one of the most read tweets, thereby attracting a lot of people to your company. Not just that, you have the chance to get people to reply to you and take advantage of feedback from them. Such an interactive session will enhance your brand's recognition and enable you to establish a strong presence on social media. When you are creating a profile page for your company, you must use an appropriate picture that speaks volumes about your company and include details about your brand that will attract people instantly.

The next platform that we looked at was YouTube. YouTube is a great place to market yourself. You saw how it is a great way to reach out to millions, and your videos will help you drive across a strong message. One of the best aspects of YouTube is its interface. It is extremely easy to create an account and upload your videos. It is even easier to view videos, so your customers will have it quite easy. Gone are the days when people relied on text advertisements. Isn't it much easier to play a video and get the message? It saves time and effort and also gets you a free demonstration of the product or service. And all of this on demand! No more waiting for your favorite ads to play on television; all it takes is clicking on the link on YouTube. Just ensure that you are using good-quality videos that were either shot by you yourself or by a professional. Once the video is up, you must view it to ensure that everything is working fine.

The next platform that we looked at was Instagram. Instagram is a very powerful tool that you can use for marketing your brand and products. Making use of high-quality pictures is a great way to showcase your products. Start by choosing the best username for your account and set up a profile that is reminiscent of your brand's image. Upload good-quality pictures that have been taken by a professional and ensure that all details are perfect. You must also make use of user-generated images in order to keep people interested. Remember to always remain interactive and reply to any queries that people have posted. Just like Twitter, you have to understand the importance of using hashtags and knowing how it can help you. One last and important thing to do is to link your Instagram account to your other social media platforms. That way, people relate with your brand better and you can combine the power of text and picture to create a unique and appealing campaign for your products and services. You must track your mentions, just as you would for your Twitter account, to see how many times you have been mentioned. You must also encourage any famous, or popular, friends of yours to promote you; that will go a long way toward building a diverse and strong customer base.

The last media site that we looked into was LinkedIn. Many people wonder if it is possible to use this platform to promote companies and products but the truth remains that it is one of the most preferred media in the world. LinkedIn helps you establish a brand image and you can use your profile to attract many customers. You have to join other groups that have something in common with your company and take part in the different debates and interactions that take place in it. You have to update your account from time to time and ensure that you are posting interesting topics. You must create new connections on a daily basis and not limit yourself to just a few people.

This is how you can make the most of social media to collect as many customers as possible.

CONCLUSION

To dominate social media marketing, you must first understand that campaigns here are more like marathons, not sprints. This social media marketing guide is designed to help you master, manipulate, and dominate social media marketing for your small business, but it is in no way a complete guide to triple your sales and transform your small business into a global brand!

To achieve such success, it will take constant learning and application of new marketing strategies, embracing emerging marketing technologies and investing a lot of time and money in getting maximum exposure for your business.

Use this guide to kickstart your social media marketing efforts, define your target audience and find out which is the most effective platform to reach them and to convert them to customers. While Facebook, Twitter, Instagram, YouTube, and LinkedIn are the top social media tools for small business to promote their products and run effective branding campaigns, not all of them are suitable for every type of business. As an entrepreneur and marketer, it is your job to research the available social media platforms, integrate effective tools, and select the most rewarding platforms to focus on to streamline your marketing campaigns and make them a success.

All the best in your social media marketing!

www.ingramcontent.com/pod-product-compliance
Lightning Source LLC
Chambersburg PA
CBHW051901170526
45168CB00001B/194